Greenhill Books

COMBAT HANDGUNS

GREENHILL MILITARY MANUALS

COMBAT HANDGUNS

GREENHILL MILITARY MANUALS

Leroy Thompson

Greenhill Books, London
Stackpole Books, Pennsylvania

This edition of **Combat Handguns**
first published 2004 by Greenhill Books,
Lionel Leventhal Limited, Park House, 1 Russell Gardens, London NW11 9NN
Email: info@greenhillbooks.com   Website: www.greenhillbooks.com
and
Stackpole Books, 5067 Ritter Road, Mechanicsburg, PA 17055, USA

British Library Cataloguing in Publication Data:
Thomson, Leroy Thompson
Combat handguns – (Greenhill military manuals)
1. Pistols I. Title 623.4'43
ISBN 1 853675768

Library of Congress Cataloging-in-Publication Data available

Edited by Anthony Saunders
Typeset by Evgenia North
Printed and bound in Singapore by Kyodo Printing Company

Contents

CZ 75	Czech Republic	78
CZ 75D PCR Compact	Czech Republic	79
CZ 83	Czech Republic	80
CZ 85 Combat	Czech Republic	81
CZ 97B	Czech Republic	82
CZ 100	Czech Republic	83
Manurhin MR73	France	84
Manurhin Special Police F1	France	85
Heckler & Koch Mk 23 SOCOM	Germany	86
Heckler & Koch P7M8	Germany	87
Heckler & Koch USP	Germany	88
Heckler & Koch USP LEM	Germany	89
Korth Combat Magnum	Germany	90
Walther P99	Germany	91
Walther PPK	Germany	92
Beretta Model 21 Bobcat	Italy	93
Beretta Model 92/M9	Italy	94
Beretta Cougar	Italy	95
Vanad P-83	Poland	96
PM	Russia	97
PSM	Russia	98
Vektor SP1	South Africa (RSA)	99
Daewoo DP51 Mk II	South Korea (ROK)	100
Llama M82	Spain	101
SIG P210	Switzerland	102
SIG P220	Switzerland	103
SIG P226	Switzerland	104
SIG P229	Switzerland	105
SIG P239	Switzerland	106
SIG P245	Switzerland	107
SIG Pro SP2340	Switzerland	108
Autauga Mk II	USA	108
Colt 1991-A1 (Government Model)	USA	110

Colt Python	USA	111
Downsizer WSP	USA	112
Kahr MK40	USA	113
Kahr PM9	USA	114
Kel-Tec P-32	USA	115
Kel-Tec P-11	USA	116
Kimber Classic Royal	USA	117
Kimber Compact CDP II	USA	118
Kimber Custom CDP II	USA	119
Kimber Custom TLE II	USA	120
Kimber Tactical Pro II	USA	121
Kimber Ultra Ten II	USA	122
Ruger GP100	USA	123
Ruger P90	USA	124
Ruger SP101	USA	125
Seecamp LWS-32	USA	126
Smith & Wesson Model 60	USA	127
Smith & Wesson Model 64	USA	128
Smith & Wesson Model 66	USA	129
Smith & Wesson Model 360PD	USA	130
Smith & Wesson Model 396 Mountain Lite	USA	131
Smith & Wesson Model 457	USA	132
Smith & Wesson Model 686+	USA	133
Smith & Wesson Sigma	USA	134
Smith & Wesson Model 3953	USA	135
Smith & Wesson Model 4566 TSW	USA	136
Smith & Wesson Model 5906	USA	137
Springfield Armory 1911A1	USA	138
Springfield Armory XD-9	USA	139

Acknowledgements

I would like to thank
the following for their assistance
in preparing this book:

Ken Choate
Chris Corino
Greg Grimes
Denny Hansen
Frank Harris
Jeff Hoffman
John Jauss
Mike Jordan
Harry Kane
Tom Knox
Greg Kramer
Mike Larsen
Jan Libourel
Shawn McCarver
T.J. Mullin
Terry Murbach
Lucretia T. Reeves
Mitch Rosen
Ed Seyffert
Jon Shoop
Kerby Smith
Tim Wegner

Chapter 1 History of the Handgun in Combat

In some ways the term 'combat handgun' may seem redundant since the handgun was developed for, and continues to be used primarily for, close combat. One of the earliest uses for the combat handgun was as a weapon to be discharged by cavalrymen after carrying out a caracole in which they rode close to the enemy, fired, then wheeled away. Because the handgun could be fired with one hand, it remained in use with mounted troops well into the twentieth century. Poland, which maintained horse cavalry until the beginning of the Second World War, even incorporated a de-cocking lever into the Radom pistol specifically to allow a rider to render the weapon safe with one hand. Other handguns developed with the cavalryman in mind included the 1892 Lebel revolver, the cylinder of which opened to the right instead of the left, thus allowing a cavalryman to hold the reins in his left hand while loading, and the M7 Roth-Steyr with a trigger system designed to lower the chances of an accidental discharge while mounted.

The handgun was also popular with riders who had to traverse roads infested with highwaymen. A pair of large horse pistols slung on the saddle offered the ability to discourage robbers, terminally if necessary. Flintlock pistols in quantities of up to four or five were carried by members of naval boarding parties and some mounted troops, especially irregulars on the Russian steppes or in the Balkans. Kentucky and Pennsylvania flintlock pistols were known for their accuracy and were carried as secondary weapons by trappers and hunters and as primary weapons by gentlemen travellers. In Europe and the southern USA, flintlock duelling pistols were sold in matched pairs for use in settling affairs of honour, while the derringer offered a highly concealable close-combat pistol.

The development of the percussion pistol increased the handgun's reliability. The pepperbox and the Colt revolver added firepower, thus making the handgun a much more formidable weapon. Large-calibre Colt, Adams, Tranter, Remington and other percussion

Because nineteenth-century revolvers were not always considered reliable some British officers chose multi-barrelled combat pistols, such as this Lancaster, for use in colonial wars. (Joe Davis)

revolvers became the choice of soldiers, lawmen and travellers. Because of the slowness of reloading, however, many carried either multiple revolvers or, in the case of the Colt, multiple cylinders already loaded. The use of the percussion revolver in combat reached its peak during the American Civil War when cavalrymen such as Mosby's Raiders armed with multiple revolvers flung a hail of lead during a charge. In the years immediately following the Civil War, too, gunfighters such as Wild Bill Hickock, who was an artist with his Colt .36 Navy revolvers, wielded the percussion revolver with deadly effect.

Although the self-contained cartridge and the revolver with a cylinder bored all the way through were in production by Smith & Wesson prior to the American Civil War, it was not until the late 1860s or early 1870s that the cartridge revolver became the dominant combat handgun. Examples produced by Colt, Smith & Wesson, Remington, Webley, Tranter, and Adams, as well as by Continental European manufacturers, became the standard for military, police and civilian defensive use. Initially, large bore, fixed-frame revolvers made by Colt, Remington, Adams, Tranter and Webley dominated but the Smith & Wesson American and Russian models as well as the Webley-Pryse and other top-break revolvers offered the possibility for a faster reload. Still, Colt's Model 1873 Single Action Army was so widely used during the last quarter of the nineteenth century on the American Frontier that it became an icon along with the Winchester lever-action rifle. It would be a mistake, however, to assume that the Single Action Army was the only revolver to see substantial use on the Frontier. Among others, the Remington 1875 Single Action Revolver and various Smith & Wesson revolvers saw substantial use.

The double-action revolver offered the ability to fire multiple shots more quickly than was generally possible with the single-action revolver, though professional gunmen who had perfected the technique of fanning could get off multiple shots from the Single Action Army very quickly. Colt's Lightning and Model 1878, as well as double-action Webley, Tranter and Adams revolvers, were the choice of military officers and

Compact Webley concealment revolvers such as these were popular throughout the late nineteenth and early twentieth centuries.

Mule skinners, such as this one on the US punitive expedition into Mexico, carried the Colt Government Model 1911 pistol. (US National Archives)

others who needed a fast-firing, powerful revolver.

Compact cartridge handguns were popular with those who needed a weapon that could be tucked into a pocket. Such models as the Smith & Wesson Safety Hammerless or Webley Royal Irish Constabulary (RIC) revolvers or the Remington Derringer combined reliability with concealability for those who carried their weapon in a pocket, boot top, purse or muff. At this point, solid-frame revolvers, such as those from Colt and Webley, and top-break models, such as those from Smith & Wesson, dominated the market for concealment weapons. However, in 1889, Colt introduced its Navy Model to be followed by various other revolvers with swing-out cylinders, thus establishing the basis for the modern combat revolver. Smith & Wesson introduced its own Hand Ejector models, as it designated revolvers with swing-out cylinders, within the next decade. Webley, however, continued to produce its military and police revolvers with the top-break action until after the Second World War.

As many European powers, as well as the USA, faced colonial conflicts during the later nineteenth and early twentieth centuries, the need for handguns with substantial stopping power, normally provided by large-calibre

bullets, was demonstrated again and again as troops faced fanatical tribesmen who took a lot of killing. The Colt 1873 and 1878 revolvers remained in service much longer than originally intended

Two combat revolvers popular with American lawmen during the early years of the twentieth century: left, a Colt New Service .45 Colt revolver; right, a Smith & Wesson .44 Special revolver.

because of the lack of stopping power displayed by the .38 Colt cartridge. The need for stopping power also influenced the adoption of the Colt .45 Automatic. British troops, who perhaps faced more colonial conflicts than any others, retained the .455 Webley revolver well into the twentieth century for a similar reason.

Another important innovation during the later years of the nineteenth century was smokeless powder, a necessary component of viable ammunition for the automatic pistol. Once smokeless powder allowed the loading of ammunition that would not rapidly foul the action, the automatic pistol could compete with the revolver. The earliest combat auto-loaders offered either high-velocity, lightweight cartridges, as in the M1896 Mauser, or very compact pocket pistols, as in the FN M1900. The M1900 Luger and M1900 Colt offered other options in powerful, self-loading service designs.

By the First World War, many of the classic military combat handguns of the twentieth century had been adopted. Germany and many other countries were using the Parabellum (Luger) pistol, Great Britain had adopted the Webley Mark VI revolver (though not until 1915), which is generally considered the best of the Webley military handguns, and the USA had adopted the Colt Government Model Automatic. Other excellent combat

handguns, including the 1896 Mauser, Colt New Service and Smith & Wesson First and Second Model Hand Ejectors, also saw service during that conflict. The Colt Army Special, which would evolve into the Colt Official Police model, and the Smith & Wesson Military & Police model, the two revolvers which in .38 Special chambering would become the classic police revolvers of the twentieth century, were also developed during the first decade of the century.

For police officers and others armed for combat who liked the .38 Special cartridge but wanted a lighter, more easily carried revolver, the Colt Police Positive Special was introduced in 1907, while the Detective Special, a variation with a 2in barrel, was introduced in 1927. The 'Dick Special' would remain for many years the standard snub-nosed revolver associated with plain-clothes investigators. Another important development among combat revolvers was the introduction in 1935 by Smith & Wesson of the .357 Magnum cartridge, which remains today the most effective combat handgun cartridge based on street shooting statistics.

Among developments in automatic pistols between the world wars, three stand out as especially important for combat handguns. Walther popularised the double-action automatic with the PP and PPK, thus offering an automatic

which shared the double-action first round capability with the service revolver. Later, the P38 would offer a double-action service pistol chambered for the 9mm Parabellum cartridge. Walther and Sauer also experimented with aluminium-framed pistols during the years prior to the Second World War, thus anticipating

During the Second World War, German troops were equipped with a wide variety of combat handguns. One of the best was the Mauser HSc.

later lightweight combat handguns. Finally, FN introduced the legendary P35, a service pistol in 9mm Parabellum which used a double-column, high-capacity magazine to allow fourteen rounds to be carried (thirteen plus one), almost twice the norm for military-calibre service autos. It should be noted that earlier Savage pocket pistols had employed a double-column magazine with a capacity of ten rounds but it was the P35, the Browning Hi-Power as it is often known, which illustrated the advantages of a police or military pistol which carried a large number of rounds. The fact the Hi-Power had one of the most comfortable grips of any combat auto was important as well in establishing the viability of high-capacity, auto-loading pistols.

The Second World War saw few innovations in combat handguns, many of the same pistols which fought the First World War being used again in the Second World War. Instead of the .455-calibre Mark VI revolver, British forces were armed with the .380-calibre Enfield Mark IV revolver, making Great Britain the last major power to retain the revolver as its principal combat handgun. However, a substantial number of Mark VI revolvers still saw service, while Colt Government Models and Inglis Browning Hi-Powers were used by British airborne and special forces personnel. Argentine

Colt's Pocket Auto was popular as a civilian and police concealment arm through the first decades of the twentieth century but was also purchased by the US Government for issue to general officers and to OSS and CIC agents during the Second World War.

Bollester-Molina and Spanish Star pistols were also issued to British forces. Clandestine operations personnel also made substantial use of specialised pistols, often fitted with a suppressor to allow them to deliver death quietly. The suppressed High Standard .22 automatic developed for the Office of Strategic Services (OSS) would still be used by US special operations forces into the Vietnam War, while the Welrod, developed for British special operations forces during the Second World War, would continue in use for decades as well. A friend of the author was, in fact,

issued a Welrod for an operation during the Vietnam War.

Another interesting special forces pistol of the Second World War was the Liberator, also sometimes known as the Woolworth Gun. Manufactured of stampings for a reported cost of $1.71,

The Liberator pistol was developed to offer an inexpensive weapon that could be dropped into occupied territory during the Second World War. (Martin Floyd)

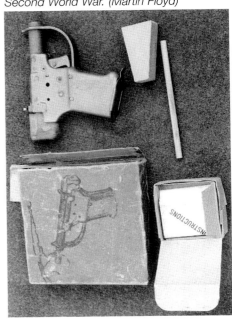

this single-shot .45 ACP pistol was intended to be dropped behind German or Japanese lines to allow resistance forces in occupied lands to kill an Axis soldier, then use the dead soldier's rifle or submachine gun.

British Commandos often carried pistols in addition to their primary weapon. In the case of this Commando Bren gunner, he has a Colt .45 auto tucked into his belt. (IWM)

The developments in combat handguns in the two decades following the Second World War were based primarily on offering lighter, more compact weapons, offering more firepower and making the handgun more durable. Soon after the war, Smith & Wesson introduced the Chief's Special, a compact five-shot .38 Special designed to be carried in the pocket. In various forms, the descendants of the Chief remain the standard for snub revolvers today. Incorporating advances in aluminium alloys, Colt introduced its Lightweight Commander, a 26oz .45 with a slightly shorter barrel. During the 1950s, Colt also introduced the .357 Magnum Python revolver, still considered by many to be the finest double-action revolver ever produced in the USA. The Smith & Wesson Combat Magnum was introduced in 1955 at the behest of lawmen who wanted a .357 Magnum revolver that was lighter than the heavy Smith & Wesson, the standard since 1935.

Outside the USA, among the most important post-war developments in combat handguns were the Makarov in the Soviet Union and the SIG P210 in Switzerland. The Makarov would become one of the most ubiquitous of all combat handguns and, with its proven Walther-based design, would provide a compact and reliable weapon throughout the

Warsaw Pact for police and military personnel. The P-210, though relatively bulky and heavy and employing a single-column magazine and single-action mechanism – all features that would seem to make it outmoded very quickly – introduced a combat handgun that was so accurate it could be used at ranges to 100yd as accurately as many other handguns could be used at 50yd.

Smith & Wesson's Model 39 self-loading pistol offered a double-action, alloy-framed 9mm for military and police use and helped open the US police market to auto-loading pistols, the first adoption being in 1961 by the Warwick, Rhode Island Police Department. Later in the 1960s, the Salt Lake City Police Department and the Illinois State Police would adopt the Model 39 as well. The French MAB P15 incorporated a double-column magazine of the type pioneered in the Browning Hi-Power but it was Smith & Wesson's Model 59 that combined double action and alloy frame with a double-column magazine. Smith & Wesson's introduction of the Model 60 stainless steel Chief's Special in 1964 was especially revolutionary as it made available a combat handgun which could ride in a pocket or holster where it was constantly exposed to perspiration, rain, salt spray or other moisture without rusting. During the Vietnam War, Model

Heckler & Koch's VP70 pioneered the use of polymer frames for combat autos.

60s were so prized that they normally sold for as much as twice their retail price.

Although the .38 Special revolver remained the primary combat revolver during the 1960s, a substantial number of lawmen and others who carried a handgun for close combat now chose the .357 Magnum revolver. A smaller number who liked revolvers that threw a larger projectile chose the .44 Special, .45 Colt, .45 ACP (carried in revolvers using half-moon clips), .41 Magnum or even .44 Magnum.

An important development during the 1970s was the Heckler & Koch VP70 which pioneered the use of a polymer frame for a combat auto-loading pistol. The SIG P220 was also introduced in the 1970s, thus establishing the SIG line of combat double-action, auto-loading handguns which remains one of the world's best and most popular lines of fighting handguns. The introduction of the Czech CZ 75 during that decade added still another excellent double-column,

double-action 9✕19 combat handgun, one that had the excellent instinctive pointing characteristics of the Browning Hi-Power but offered the option of carrying in either the double-action or single-action, cocked-and-locked mode.

By the 1980s, as US law enforcement agencies begin switching to auto-loading pistols in large numbers and the US armed forces adopted the Beretta 92 pistol, an array of innovative and functional auto-loading combat pistols became available. Heckler & Koch's P7 incorporated a versatile squeeze cocker, while Glock's use of a polymer frame and fast-action trigger would soon make it the dominant combat pistol in the world. Innovative designs from Beretta, SIG and Walther offered military and law enforcement agencies a menu of excellent combat pistols. Smith & Wesson improved its line of automatic pistols with its third-generation designs as well as offering the Sigma to compete with European polymer-framed, fast-action pistols. In fact, the development of various types of fast action has allowed the automatic pistol to be safer when being carried ready for immediate employment. Another trend in more recent military combat auto-loaders has been towards the very high velocity, small-calibre cartridge designed to defeat body armour. The Russian PAM and the

Belgian FN Five-seveN® are two good examples of this type of pistol.

European firearms manufacturers, traditionally wedded to the automatic pistol, surprisingly offered two of the finest revolvers ever produced: the French Manurhin and the German Korth. Over the last decade, the use of new materials in revolvers from Smith & Wesson and Taurus has made the 'wheel

The Glock offered many revolutionary improvements to the combat pistol and has become the world's standard by which other fighting handguns are evaluated.

gun' a viable combat arm once again, especially in lightweight, powerful pocket guns chambered for the .38 Special or .357 Magnum round. Revolvers, such as Smith & Wesson's M360 which fires the .357 Magnum cartridge but weighs just over 12oz, offer a lot of power which can ride in a trousers or jacket pocket. Smith & Wesson has also attempted to compete with powerful auto-loading pistols by increasing the cartridge capacity of some of its .357 Magnum revolvers, employing a seven-shot cylinder on the Model 686+ and an eight-shot cylinder on the Model 27-7.

Research continues into 'smart guns' which will be coded to their user's DNA to prevent their unauthorised use. The use of tritium night sights as well as laser sights and white-light illuminators has made the combat handgun even more effective at night.

Despite all of the developments in combat handguns over the last century, however, the basic revolver and auto-loading pistol remain the primary choices for those needing to arm themselves with a sidearm. In fact, despite all of the advances in design and materials, if you found yourself in harm's way armed with a Colt 1873 Single Action Army, a Webley Mark VI, a Mauser 1896 or a Colt 1911 Government Model you would still be able to defend yourself quite well. The

designers who created the modern combat handgun at the end of the nineteenth and beginning of the twentieth centuries did an excellent job. For the most part, modern combat handguns are just evolutionary descendants of those original fighting sidearms.

Chapter 2 Missions of the Combat Handgun

At first glance, there appears to be a diverse array of combat handguns available and you might ask why that is. The answer is not simple. Combat handguns are required to perform myriad tasks and rarely will one handgun perform more than a few of them well. There is also an element of personal preference which should be given consideration since the combat handgun is a very personal weapon. In this chapter, an attempt will be made to delineate the primary tasks of the combat handgun and to explain what types of handgun will normally perform those tasks most effectively.

Worldwide, perhaps the most ubiquitous use of the combat handgun is as the sidearm for uniformed police officers. Although in the past many police agencies chose revolvers for their officers, overwhelmingly today this task is fulfilled by the auto-loading pistol. To perform its task effectively, the standard police duty pistol must combine a range of features, some of which are somewhat contradictory. For example, the police pistol must be capable of instant deployment in case the officer unexpectedly confronts an armed felon, yet it must also be very safe to lower the

likelihood of an accidental discharge which can endanger the officer, colleagues or innocent bystanders. Various innovations have allowed the police pistol to meet both of these criteria. For example, the Glock fast-action design is very quick to bring into action, yet its trigger design is such that the pistol will withstand a drop from a multi-story building without going off. However, the fast-action design requires officers to be well trained to keep their finger off the trigger except when they intend to fire. It also requires a holster that covers the trigger guard. Double-action only (DOA) pistols also address the need for both speed of deployment and safety as the double action allows a rapid first shot, while this type of action eliminates the circumstance of a cocked pistol, unlike with a single-action pistol. Variations on the fast or double action from Walther, Smith & Wesson, Heckler & Koch and SIG have all achieved some success as police pistols.

The police pistol must also be highly reliable and durable. A police pistol must be so well designed and so well constructed that it can ride on the belt for years, only being drawn for qualification shooting, yet still be ready to perform

Large-calibre handguns, such as this Smith & Wesson Model 24 .44 Special, may be carried for defence against man or beast.

when the officer needs it in an emergency. With auto-loading pistols, a key element is that the pistol will function reliably with any ammunition likely to be used in it. As a result, agencies will normally fire thousands of rounds through a pistol being considered for adoption. Fortunately, most of the current group of popular auto-loading pistols have been designed to function reliably with hollow-pointed combat ammunition. The Beretta Model 92, SIG 226, SIG 228 and Glock Model 17 and variants have been adopted by enough law enforcement agencies and military forces that the designs have passed rigorous performance testing. Glocks have an especially fine reputation for durability, examples used on police or military training ranges often having fired hundreds of thousands of rounds with only minor maintenance. Note, too, that a strong point of the Glock's design for law enforcement is that it has few parts and any that are likely to break may be easily replaced if they do.

Another aspect of durability is that the police pistol must be capable of standing up to the elements when carried in an exposed holster. Stainless steel construction is one feature which adds durability. In some cases, stainless steel may be made even more durable by adding finishes such as Melonite or RoGuard. The use of polymers, as in the Glock, Walther P99, S&W Sigma, H&K USP and Beretta Vertec, also enhances durability. Fabrication using titanium or scandium not only aids durability but also substantially lightens the handgun to make it easier to carry. So far, lightweight alloys of these metals have been used primarily for revolvers, though Taurus offers a 9mm auto and other companies will soon introduce auto-loading pistols that use a substantial amount of titanium or scandium.

Since the police pistol will be used by a varied group of individuals, of varying sizes, the duty sidearm must be as ergonomic as possible. Grip size is one important feature. With the Glock, for example, some shooters find that the size of grip on the Model 19 is comfortable, while the grip on the Model 17 is not. Others can handle both of these grips but find that the grips of the Model 20 and Model 21 are too large.

Military and police hostage rescue teams often use handguns for clearing buildings. In this case, US Army personnel practice their techniques in a tyre house.

For agencies which issue the Glock, some allow smaller shooters to choose the smaller version, chambered for the same round. Another option is to send the weapon to ROBAR, an Arizona-based company that will slim the Glock grip to allow comfortable use by those with

Suppressed pistols may be used for silently eliminating enemy sentries or taking out lights during an assault.

smaller hands. The Walther P99 offers another solution as it comes with three different sizes of interchangeable grip to allow for small, medium and large hands.

Another feature which is important on the police duty pistol is the safety system. Pistols such as the Glock, S&W Sigma, Walther P99 and H&K USP which require no external safety are preferred by many law enforcement agencies since they are ready for action by just pulling the trigger. On pistols such as the standard Smith & Wesson third-generation models, the Beretta 92 and the SIG P220 series, there are two basic types of hammer-drop safety. Additionally, these pistols are all available in self-cocking or double-action-only mode. The two basic safeties are the Smith & Wesson-type, which may be used to drop the hammer, with the gun then left in the safe position, and the SIG-type, which allows the hammer to drop and automatically returns the gun to the ready mode. This device is sometimes referred to as a de-cocker rather than a safety. There are arguments for both types. Those who like their handgun to be left on safe argue that this type of safety device means that a criminal snatching the weapon from the officer will not immediately be able to turn it against him. There is validity to this argument as there are police officers who have lost their weapons and survived

because the assailant could not figure out how to make the weapon work. An additional advantage of this type of safety is that it allows the pistol to be loaded and a round chambered without ever having the hammer cocked. The downside of this type of safety is that under stress an officer may forget to flick the safety off. The SIG-type safety device eliminates this possibility but during the loading process it does leave the hammer cocked on a loaded chamber until the hammer-drop safety is operated. This type of safety also allows an assailant to snatch a weapon and instantly turn it on its owner.

There are other safety systems which may be encountered. The CZ 75, for example, incorporates a safety that locks the hammer in typical single-action mode.

A popular police second gun for many years was this High-Standard .22 derringer.

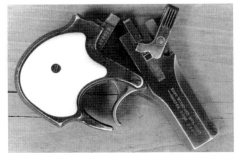

A US soldier with General Pershing in Mexico carries a Colt 1911 automatic. (US National Archives)

However, when the pistol is used in double-action mode, it is necessary to drop the hammer by pulling the trigger and easing the hammer down with the thumb, a method which increases the chance of an accidental discharge. The H&K P7 incorporates a squeeze-cocker safety which prevents the weapon from firing unless the cocker is squeezed by the shooting hand. This is a fast system which contributes to accuracy but those using the P7 must be very well trained to release the pressure on the squeeze-cocker when moving with the weapon or when reholstering it.

Sights are another important consideration with the law enforcement handgun. Trainers disagree on whether it is better to have fixed sights or adjustable sights. The argument for fixed sights is that an armourer can get them set for the duty load, thus eliminating the possibility of an officer messing up the sights. On the other hand, adjustable sights offer more versatility. Normally, it is most important that the sights allow rapid acquisition of a target so that the weapon may be quickly brought on to the target. Many law enforcement agencies also want tritium night sights to make the weapon more effective in darkness when a substantial percentage of police shooting engagements take place. Certainly for special police units, and in

some cases for all personnel, agencies today prefer handguns with rails to take white-light illuminators or laser targeting systems.

The police handgun for plain-clothes investigators will often be the same weapon used by uniformed personnel but it is often deemed desirable to have a more compact model which is easier to conceal and offers a higher status. In

Germany's GSG-9 counter-terrorist unit chose the H&K P7 as a backup to their MP5 submachine guns.

some cases, a more compact version of the standard weapon used by uniformed officers will be adopted for investigators. For example, if the Glock 17 is the standard duty weapon, the more compact Glock 19 or Glock 26 might serve for investigators. For agencies using the SIG P226 or P228, the SIG P239 offers a slimmer and more compact weapon. Often, a more important consideration for investigators than the size of the weapon is that the proper holster is chosen and that the weapon is designed so that its sights or sharp edges will not snag on a jacket.

Some specialised law enforcement personnel require special handguns. Undercover narcotics officers, for example, want very compact weapons or full-sized weapons which do not look like 'cop guns.' In the USA, at least, officers who enforce game or wildlife laws may chose a weapon for use against felons but which retains the capability of stopping a bear if necessary. Although most officers involved in enforcing wildlife regulations will also carry a rifle in their vehicle, they may still choose a powerful handgun such as a Smith & Wesson .44 Magnum revolver or a Glock 20 10mm automatic. SWAT officers will often choose handguns similar to those carried by military special operations personnel. Their handguns may have also had some custom work to enhance their accuracy.

Military handguns share many features with law enforcement handguns. Durability is an obvious necessity – one reason that handguns adopted for military use generally go through rigorous reliability and durability testing. Although law enforcement agencies normally prefer high-capacity, auto-loading pistols, this feature is deemed especially desirable in a military pistol since it grants more sustained firepower and allows the soldier to carry fewer spare magazine for the pistol. In military use, the handgun is the primary weapon for high-ranking officers, aircrew, technical specialists and many crew-served weapons operators. As a result, it may be desirable to have a weapon with capability of engagement to 50yd or even further. The FN Five-seveN® pistol employs a very flat shooting round which can be fired accurately to even 100yd or more with practice. The Five-seveN® round will also penetrate ballistic helmets

Pistols are often the primary arm for armoured crewmen or, in the case of these German paratroopers, the weapon with which they jumped. (Bundesarchiv)

Members of France's GIGN counter-terrorist unit practicing with their Manurhin MR73 revolvers. (ECP)

and vests, making it much more effective as a combat round than its lightweight bullet might indicate. Additionally, the pistol is lightweight yet incorporates a very high capacity magazine. Many view the FN Five-seveN® as the military pistol of the future.

Another important feature of the military pistol is ease of disassembly for field maintenance. As an adjunct to ease of disassembly, it is also desirable if the number of parts that may be readily removed is few to help 'soldier-proof' the weapon and lessen the possibility of losing parts. Those handguns which incorporate a modular hammer/action assembly such as the SIG P210 retain the small parts in the one assembly and allow ease of maintenance. The use of polymer frames, stainless steel

components or special finishes such as Melonite enhance the durability of military handguns as well.

Although military units in some countries will adopt a locally made handgun out of ethnocentrism, most of the world's armed forces are satisfied with one of a narrow range of handguns. Most widely used are the Beretta 92 (in US issue, the M9), the Glock, the Colt Government Model, the Makarov and the Browning Hi-Power.

In some cases, too, there will be one handgun for conventional forces and a second handgun – or sometimes multiple additional handguns – for special operations forces. Combat swimmers, for example, often need a specialised pistol. Heckler & Koch has produced various

The handgun will often be the choice for hostage rescue operations in confined spaces as in this bus assault.

designs for use by combat swimmers, while the Sub-Aqua Glock is a standard Glock 17 with a special firing-pin cup to allow it to be fired under water. Suppressed pistols are also widely used by special operations forces. The Heckler & Koch Mark 23 is a .45 ACP pistol designed specifically for special operations. In addition to being designed to take a suppressor, it incorporates rails for various types of illumination/sighting devices.

Still another mission of the combat handgun is for civilian self-defence. In countries which allow civilians to own handguns for self-defence, such handguns may be broken down into two basic groups: those which are carried on the person and those which are kept in the home or business premises. Those

US Army personnel practicing bus assaults. Note that the last man has a pistol.

carried on the person are normally chosen for their ease of concealment so as not to attract attention to their user. Compact, lightweight pistols such as the

Members of the Special Air Service practice assaults on a train. Note the Browning Hi-Power pistols carried on their thighs as back-up weapons. Note also that they carry an extension magazine in the pistol. (22nd SAS)

Glock 26 and Glock 27, the Para-Ordnance P-10 and P-12, the Colt Light Weight Commander, the Smith & Wesson Ladysmith series of autos and revolvers, the Walther PPK, Smith & Wesson and Taurus titanium or scandium revolvers and deep concealment pistols such as the Seecamp LWS-32 are all designed for such use.

Those handguns that are kept at home or at a business may be full-sized service weapons, though, if small children are in a home, a great deal of consideration must be given to safety features. Taurus revolvers, for example, incorporate a lock in the weapon which locks the action and can only be unlocked with a key supplied with the revolver. This enhances safety but it can make deploying the weapon in an emergency time-consuming. Some users keep the revolver locked and unloaded at all times except at night when they load it, unlock it and place it next to the bed. Other handguns incorporate built-in locking systems or magazine safeties which render the pistol inoperable if the magazine is removed. Still another consideration for self-defence weapons is that many countries have laws governing what type of weapon or calibre may be used by civilians. In some cases, the maximum calibre of revolver that may be used is .38 Special, while the maximum

US special operations personnel often carry a Beretta M9 in addition to their M4 carbines.

calibre of auto-loading pistol may be .380 ACP. Other countries limit self-defence weapons to .32 calibre or lower.

Fortunately, excellent handguns are available to fit any of these missions. Some are proven designs which have been around for almost a century, while others incorporate the latest in high-tech materials and design. The final consideration is that the handgun can deliver enough power to immediately stop an assailant, can do so accurately out to 25yd or more, can do so reliably and can be kept safely near at hand.

Chapter 3 Maximising the Combat Handgun

Although today's combat handguns are arguably the best ever, there are still specialist gunsmiths and armourers who attempt to maximise the potential of the weapons. Often, in fact, today's custom features become the standard within the following decade as firearms manufacturers take note of improvements on custom models.

One of the most common alterations to the combat handgun is what is usually known as an 'action job.' Designed to make the trigger pull smoother and lighter so that the pistol or revolver may be held

The two ports cut into the slide and barrel of this Glock 23C help dampen recoil and allow faster shooting.

on target during the trigger squeeze, the action job usually consists of polishing trigger and sear parts and other smoothing of the action mechanism. Because of the design of the Glock, armourers can easily adjust the trigger pull by changing a few parts. The standard Glock trigger pull is 5lb but it may be lowered to 3.5lb with a simple change of parts. Some agencies issuing the Glock go in the other direction and increase the 5lb pull to lesson the chance of an accidental discharge. A few weapons, such as the Korth revolver, allow

The enhanced grip safety on this Para-Ordnance pistol both protects the hand from 'hammer bite' and also allows the web of the hand to depress it completely.

the shooter to easily adjust the trigger pull to fit his own preferences.

Another common custom procedure is designed to enhance the reliability of

Combat revolver grips should incorporate a cut-out to allow the use of a speed-loader.

auto-loading pistols, including polishing the feed ramp, throating the chamber, polishing the slide rails and changing the springs. Wolf Springs is a company which specialises in producing high-quality auto-pistol springs. The magazine well may be bevelled as well to allow the magazine to be fitted more surely during a rapid reload, while the magazine itself may be fitted with rubber 'slam pads' to allow it to be thrust home more surely during the reload. Reliability work on revolvers usually consists of adjusting the timing so the cylinders line up more precisely and slightly throating the chambers of the cylinder so that speed loaders may be used more reliably. The addition of an ambidextrous safety on auto-loading pistols allows the weapon to be used with either hand should the

Eagle Secret Service grips above and Spegel Boot Grips below, two of the most ergonomic combat grips for the fighting revolver.

primary shooting hand be injured. Some users also like to deactivate magazine safeties that prevent the weapon from being fired without the magazine in place,

so that the round in the chamber can be fired during a reload.

Another group of custom procedures is designed to allow the weapon to be carried concealed more readily and be quickly drawn and brought into action. Normally, this will consist of rounding off any sharp edges. On some weapons, the hammer spur may be removed or bobbed. Rear sights will often be rounded as well.

A simple but very important method for tailoring a combat handgun to its user is to add special grips. Weapons such as the Walther P99 incorporate the capability of changing grips to enhance its usefulness but, in the case of most handguns, it will be necessary to add after-market grips. The author, for example, normally

Elephant ivory combat grips from Ajax Grips for an engraved S&W revolver.

The author likes to replace factory S&W revolver grips with these combat grips from Craig Spegel.

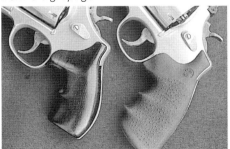

Combat handguns may be enhanced with special grips such as these stag grips from Eagle Grips.

changes factory revolver grips for more ergonomic ones from Eagle Grips (www.eaglegrips.com), Ajax Grips (www.ajaxgrips.com) or Craig Spegel. Eagle's Secret Service grips and Spegel's boot grips are among the best for revolvers. Craig Spegel also makes excellent grips for the Browning Hi-Power.

Another simple method to enhance the effectiveness of the combat handgun is to make its sighting system more effective. Replacing narrow rear sights with combat sights having a wider notch is one popular modification. Novak combat rear sights were at one time a common custom option but are now offered as standard on many auto-loading pistols. The inclusion of white

One of the most useful enhancements for the police or military combat handgun is the mounting of a laser or a light.

Another easy method of adding laser capability is through the use of Laser Grips which incorporate the laser in the grip of the handgun. (Crimson Trace)

The LaserMax system allows a laser to be attached by replacing the pistol's guide rod, thus eliminating the need for any external attachments.

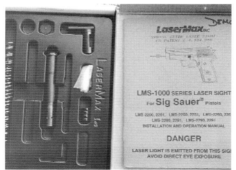

dots or a combination of a dot and bar on front and rear sights also aids in rapid alignment. Night sights such as those from Trijicon allow the handgun to be used more effectively at night. In some cases, too, adjustable sights are desirable to aid in adjusting them to the bullet's point of impact. When choosing adjustable sights, however, it is important to avoid target-style sights which are so bulky that they might snag during a draw.

Still another boon in sighting, especially at night, is the addition of a white light or laser. Many current automatic pistols incorporate a rail on the frame specifically designed to take such devices. For those that do not, there are other options. Crimson Trace

The LaserMax laser system installed on a SIG P245. (LaserMax)

offers a line of Laser Grips which replace the standard grips on the handgun but incorporate a laser aiming device. LaserMax offers a compact laser system which replaces the guide rod for the recoil spring on Glock and SIG pistols and some others. Excellent aiming devices that fit on to the frame-mounted rails are available from Insight Technology and Surefire. Insight Technology offers variations of its versatile LAM (Laser Aiming Module) which are very compact yet offer a combination of laser, white light and infrared illumination. The LAM is particularly useful for military and police special operations use.

Smith & Wesson 4566 TSW with Insight Technology Tactical Illuminator attached. The carrying case for the illuminator is from De Santis.

Perhaps the best idea of what a full customising package on a combat handgun consists of can be gained from the specifications for a ROBAR Super Deluxe Government Model .45 automatic. Features include:

- silver-soldered Bo-Mar rear sight with a dovetail front sight using a Novak blank
- flattened and stippled slide top
- cocking serrations to the front of the slide
- serrations on the back of the slide
- ambidextrous safety
- lightweight trigger
- chequered magazine release
- chequered front strap and mainspring housing
- custom stocks and grip screws
- beaver-tail grip safety
- commander hammer
- match sear
- spring kit and guide rod
- match-grade barrel and bushing
- barrel throating and polished feed ramp
- full trigger job
- dehorning to eliminate sharp edges
- lowered and flared ejection port
- tuned extractor
- polished breech face
- relieved frame to allow a higher grip
- extended ejector

- tightened slide for a better fit to the frame
- test fired for function and accuracy
- high-durability finish such as NP3 or Roguard/NP3

As mentioned above, in many cases, custom features such as those incorporated into a ROBAR pistol will be more than the average soldier or police officer will need. However, pistols carried by special operations units tasked with hostage rescue or other missions may be customised to maximise the capabilities of the weapons. In some cases, too, the pistol maximised for 'street combat' might

Handguns from the Kimber Custom Shop, such as this Compact CDP II, display many of the features deemed essential to maximise the combat handgun, including ambidextrous oversized safety, skele-tonised hammer and beaver-tail safety.

incorporate many, but not all, of these features. Instead of the relatively large Bo-Mar adjustable rear sight, for example, Robar's high-visibility, low-profile rear sight might be more desirable.

In considering custom features for the combat handgun, though, it must be remembered that alterations are always a trade-off. Tightening the slide and carrying out other operations to enhance accuracy must not make the pistol less reliable and the addition of sophisticated sighting devices must not make the weapon so bulky that it is no longer portable. The great value of the combat handgun is its propinquity. Its user must be willing to keep it close at hand and be confident that it will perform reliably and accurately every time it is drawn.

ROBAR customised Browning Hi-Power. (ROBAR)

Combat rear sights with three dots or tritium inserts are an important aid in rapid target acquisition. These are on a Para-Ordnance pistol.

Chapter 4 **Carrying the Combat Handgun**

For the combat handgun to be effective it must be available when needed. Hence, the importance of how it is carried and the holster. The combat holster must combine various characteristics to perform its job. It must protect the weapon from the elements and keep it secure so that it does not fall out or, in the case of the police holster, allow an assailant to easily snatch it, yet it must also allow the weapon to be brought quickly into action. The holster must also retain the weapon safely by covering the trigger without applying pressure to the hammer or safety.

Typical police duty rig for the Beretta Model 92 pistol. Note the horizontal spare magazine pouch.

The military holster puts its greatest emphasis on protecting the weapon since the handgun will rarely be the primary weapon for military personnel. Currently, military holsters are normally constructed of polymer materials with nylon to offer greater resistance to the elements. A good example is Bianchi's UM92 Universal Military holster. Designed for the US armed forces to carry the M9 Beretta, it is can be adapted for either right-handed or left-handed wear, fitted with a Tactical Hip Extender for special operations use or for personnel who may need access while seated, adapted for a chest or underarm harness and easily fitted with a thumb-snap system. Although originally designed for the Beretta M9, it is offered for most popular military autos.

For special operations use, Eagle Industries and Blade Tech, among others, offer specialised drop holsters which will take weapons fitted with lasers, white-light illuminators, suppressors and other accessories. Many of these holsters incorporate a spare magazine pouch. The Eagle model is fabricated of tough black or olive drab ballistic nylon, while the Blade-Tech version is constructed of a thermoplastic moulded to the weapon.

Eagle Industries offers a wide variety of special operations holsters specifically designed for helicopter pilots, combat swimmers and others.

Uniformed police duty rigs are designed for the overt carrying of the weapon and must keep it secure while allowing ease of access. Although a few

Aker duty holster for a SIG P229 pistol.

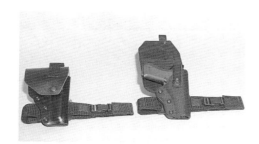

De Santis Tactical Duty Holster originally designed for the NYPD Emergency Services Unit. (De Santis)

agencies still require officers to wear covered holsters with flaps, most now choose open-top holsters. In many cases, as well, safety straps have been eliminated in favour of a holster which retains the weapon through a built in retention device. Bianchi, for example, uses a 'pinch' retention device. Many designs incorporate a tension screw which allows the officer to tighten the holster to the point where the weapon is retained but may still be drawn quickly. Police duty holsters are designed to be part of a full duty rig, often consisting of a heavy-duty belt, holster, spare magazine pouches, handcuff carrying case, baton holder, pepper spray holder, radio carrier, torch pouch, key carrier and keepers, the latter designed to anchor the belt in place. Some agencies still use a Sam

Browne belt to help carry the weight of the duty rig. Many makers around the world offer police duty rigs. Among the best from the USA are Aker, Bianchi, De Santis, and Gould and Goodrich.

Whether among off-duty or plain-clothes law enforcement personnel, military personnel operating in civilian attire or armed civilians perhaps the most popular type of concealment holster is what is usually known as the strong-side hip holster. 'Strong side' designates that it

Ken Null belt holster for the FN Five-seveN®.

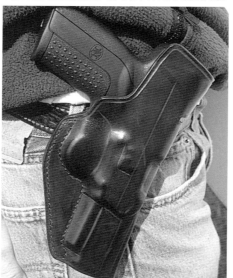

is positioned on the same side as the shooting hand. A wide array of styles and materials are available for the hip holster. When ordering one, the wearer must first choose the width of belt on which it will be worn. Gun belts are available in widths from 1–2 in, though most concealment holsters are designed for belts of 1–1$\frac{1}{2}$ in. Often, these belts are of double thickness or incorporate a metal or plastic insert to stiffen them and anchor the weapon in position. The holster's belt loop is also important. Many like a split loop which allows the holster to be positioned with a trousers belt loop between the holster loops thus anchoring the holster. Paddle holsters are popular with plain-clothes law enforcement personnel since they allow the weapon to be easily removed for

Galco shark-skin holster and belt combination makes a handsome accompaniment to an engraved S&W Model 49 with ivory grips.

desk storage when in the office. Snap belt loops also allow ease of removal.

Another important choice will be the cant of the holster. Many like the FBI rake which positions the butt for a faster draw but others may prefer a neutral rake.

Although the traditional material for holsters has been cow hide, many other materials are available. Horse hide is preferred by many because of its durability, while others like shark skin because it is durable and attractive. For those wanting more exotic materials, ostrich, alligator and crocodile are available. Among more modern materials are Kydex and ballistic nylon.

Many manufacturers offer high-quality hip holsters. Among the author's favourites are those from Blade-Tech, which, for military personnel, are available in various camouflage patterns. These Kydex or Concealex holsters retain the weapon well and are comfortable but also allow very fast

Attractive and functional Basket Weave 1930 Austin holster and belt rig from El Paso Saddlery for a 4in S&W .44 Special revolver. El Paso offers traditional holsters for a wide range of combat handguns.

access. They are also virtually indestructible. Fobus, an Israeli firm, makes a line of very effective injection-moulded holsters which are inexpensive yet extremely well designed and well made. The author also likes the very traditional hip holsters from El Paso Saddlery which offers many designs that have been used for decades by Texas Rangers and other western lawmen but which are still highly usable and extremely attractive. El Paso offers traditional basket, floral and other types of carving and makes an extremely handsome dress rig. Another maker of traditional hip holsters, Bell Charter-Oak, produces the designs of Chic Gaylord, including the Federal Speed Scabbard

Mitch Rosen shark-skin inside-the-waistband holster for a presentation Browning Hi-Power.

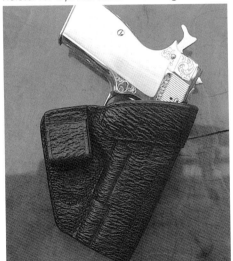

Blade-Tech's camouflage holsters are excellent for military use.

popular with FBI agents during the 1950s and 1960s. One of the makers of the highest quality holster in the world is Mitch Rosen Gunleather, which offers an excellent line of hip holsters, including a group specifically designed for female users. Among other makers of well-designed hip holsters are Ken Null, De Santis, Ted Blocker, Thad Rybka and Milt Sparks. Among those from Milt Sparks, the author especially likes the Nelson Legacy and the PMK for revolvers.

An interesting variation on the hip holster is available from BCO (Bell Charter Oak). BCO offers a double hip holster which positions one holster behind the strong-side hip and the other in front of it. Designed originally for New York City detectives who often carry two

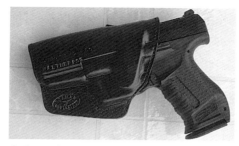

Bullman Secret Agent IWB holster for the Walther P99.

guns, this rig has two styles. One positions the forward gun for a cross draw with the weak hand or 'cavalry' draw with the strong hand, while the second gun is positioned for a traditional

strong-side draw. The other variation positions both guns for the strong-side draw, one in front of the other. Although this rig takes some getting used to for comfort, it is a viable option for those who perform law enforcement duties in a dangerous environment.

A popular variation on the strong-side hip holster when greater concealment is desired is the inside-the-waistband (IWB) holster, also designed to be worn on the strong side at the hip. The IWB holster has the advantage of placing the portion of the holster containing the barrel inside the trousers, thus allowing a short jacket to conceal the weapon. For such rigs to be comfortable, however, the holster must use thin material and be positioned perfectly. Blade-Tech's IWB model takes

Blade-Tech SWAT drop holster for a Glock with Insight Technology M6 Illuminator attached.

Bell Charter Oak dual rig designed to carry primary and back-up guns on the strong side. This rig is popular with New York City detectives.

This Bell Charter Oak GNS is designed for those who carry big-bore revolvers for combat.

advantage of its construction in Kydex or Concealex to create a thin holster which offers great retention and speed. Other IWB models which the author has found especially effective are the ARG from Mitch Rosen, the Heritage and Summer Special from Milt Sparks, the Secret Agent and the Secret Agent (thin) from Bulman Gunleather, the Extreme Heat and Summer Heat from Wild Bill's, the

Blade-Tech makes holsters in the same colours as Levis to allow a holster to blend in when wearing casual clothes.

PCCH from Don Hume and the Royal Guard and Summer Comfort from Galco. Uncle Bill's and Mitch Rosen also offer a specialised 'tuckable' holster which has some aspects of the IWB but is designed for the shirt to be bloused over the weapon to conceal it but allows fast access.

Not all belt holsters are strong-side designs, however. The cross draw, for example, positions the weapon in front of the weak-side hip for a draw with the shooting hand. The cross draw is especially fast for those who are seated such as VIP drivers, helicopter pilots and harbour police. The cross draw also allows the weapon to be protected with the weak-side elbow while moving through crowds, an advantage for those in VIP protection. On the negative side,

the cross draw presents the weapon's butt to anyone who might attempt to snatch the weapon. Among holster makers who make effective cross-draw holsters are Kramer Handgun Leather, Galco, Ted Blocker, El Paso Saddlery (the 1920 Crossdraw model), Ken Null, and Mitch Rosen. Null's VAM and

Blade-Tech's Kydex inside-the-waistband holster is the most comfortable of this type.

Kramer cross-draw holster for large automatics.

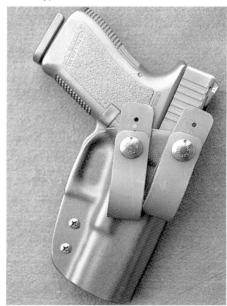

Mitch Rosen's Counter Carjack Rig places the gun in the position for a draw while seated in a vehicle.

Rosen's CCR (Counter Carjacking Rig) are specifically designed for VIP drivers or others who may need to access their weapon quickly while seated in a vehicle. The author also especially likes Galco's Cover Six.

A style of concealment belt rig favoured by some but which the author finds uncomfortable is the small-of-the-back rig. Designed to fit into the hollow of the back for better concealment and canted at an angle to allow ease of draw, these holsters offer excellent concealment. Among the best are those from Don Hume, Galco, Aker, Horseshoe Leather and De Santis. Although the author does not usually wear this type of rig because he does not find it comfortable, he is also concerned about the effect it might have on his spine if he were wearing it in a traffic accident. Not only that, when he has worn one, he has always felt uncomfortable when standing in a queue with someone close behind since, even though the weapon is concealed; the person could very easily snatch it.

Another group of holsters are designed to conceal the handgun without having to wear a gun belt. One of the most popular of these concealment holsters is the side- or hip-pocket holster. The side-pocket holster positions the weapon in the side pocket for ease of draw when the hand is thrust into the pocket. If the handgun carried in the pocket is the primary weapon, it will normally be carried on the same side as the shooting hand but, if it is carried as a secondary weapon, many like to carry it in the weak-side pocket for access if the primary hand or arm is injured or in case the user is engaged in a struggle for the primary weapon. It is amazing how the fight goes out of someone struggling for your weapon when another handgun is suddenly stuck in his ear!

Many pocket holsters incorporate some method of keeping the holster in place during the draw. For example, those from Thad Rybka utilise a nub at the top of the front of the holster on which the drawer presses down with the thumb while drawing. Others fabricate the holster with the rough side facing outwards so that friction against the pocket lining helps keep it in place. Milt Sparks uses a malleable wire frame moulded into the leather which allows the

Kramer's Explorer holster offers a flap for those who carry their weapon into tough climates.

Aker's side-pocket holster incorporates an outer flap to break up the profile of the weapon in the pocket.

holster to be fitted to the pocket once it is inserted. De Santis takes still another approach with The Nemesis which utilises material which is 'sticky' to keep it in place and a foam core to break up the weapon's outline.

Thad Rybka's side-pocket holster incorporates a nub against which the thumb presses when drawing the pistol. This not only aids the draw but keeps the holster in the pocket.

To effectively conceal the weapon, the pocket holster must be designed so that it breaks up the handgun's profile. Aker Leather does this effectively by incorporating a flap on the outside of the pocket holster. In addition to concealing the handgun, the pocket holster should also protect it within the pocket from lint, change, keys and anything else that might be in there. In the case of a pocket automatic with an exposed hammer, the pocket holster should also allow the weapon to be safely carried without the safety being inadvertently worked into the 'fire' position.

In addition to the makers already mentioned, the author has used good pocket holsters from Ken Null, Mitch Rosen, De Santis, Ted Blocker and Kramer Handgun Leather.

This Milt Sparks pocket holster incorporates a wire frame which may be fitted to the pocket for better concealment.

There are other types of holster apart from those already discussed. For example, Don Hume offers a holster designed for the hip pocket. In the past, many US police officers used a hip-pocket holster designed to look like a wallet to carry a High Standard derringer as a back-up weapon. This holster was

Aker holster designed to carry a back-up gun on the ballistic vest.

Mitch Rosen's Pocket Cozy, a vertical pocket holster for windbreakers or other jackets which require a vertical draw.

designed to allow the derringer to be fired while still in the holster. Mitch Rosen offers the Cozy, a holster designed for patch pockets as on windbreakers, jackets or cargo trousers. Another type of pocket holster is actually designed into the pocket. Some police departments, for example, have used duty trousers with a leather holster pocket sewn into them, while others have issued winter coats with a leather holster built into the external pocket for ease of access in cold weather when the coat is buttoned over a standard hip holster.

A very popular method of carrying a concealed weapon, used by undercover police officers and intelligence agents, is the ankle holster. At one point, in fact, the military officer accompanying the President of the USA with the 'Football',

the nuclear launch codes, carried his weapon in this manner. For an ankle holster to be used effectively it is normally worn on the weak-side ankle so that it can be easily drawn with the gun hand. To avoid hopping around on one leg, one technique for the draw is to go down on the knee opposite the ankle holster while drawing. This also makes the user a smaller target during the draw and takes advantage of the tendency to shoot high when under stress.

Normally, leather ankle holsters incorporate padding around the ankle for comfort, while those constructed of ballistic nylon normally do not need padding. Eagle Industries offers some very comfortable and well-designed ankle holsters, including one which positions the weapon upside down and incorporates a pouch for a spare

Wild Bill's Extreme Heat IWB holster for the Browning Hi-Power.

magazine. Bianchi's Triad ankle holster is constructed of nylon but also incorporates a pad for comfort. This holster has the reputation for staying in place very well. Other popular ankle holsters are available from Mitch Rosen, Don Hume, Gould and Goodrich, Kramer, Galco and De Santis. Note that De Santis makes a group of ankle holsters especially designed for compact Glock

Bianchi ankle holster allows concealment of relatively large autos.

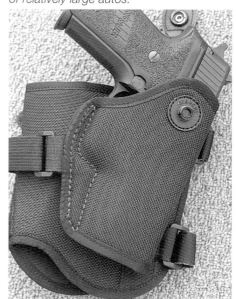

autos. Since such a large number of law enforcement agencies use the Glock, this is a real boon. The compact Glock 26 or Glock 27 is the best choice for carrying in an ankle holster. The author has never found the ankle holster as comfortable as a pocket holster or other types of concealment holsters. However, this is

Eagle Industries ankle holster allows a relatively large handgun, such as this Glock 27, to be carried concealed beneath the trousers leg.

one of the best methods of carrying a concealed handgun.

Another type of holster used predominantly by those in law enforcement is one designed to be attached to the ballistic vest to hold a second 'hideout' or back-up gun. Aker and Uncle Mike's produce this type of holster which is designed to attach to the vest's straps. The latest generation of Smith & Wesson and Taurus lightweight snub-nosed revolvers carry very well in this way as do the Glock 26 and Glock 27 and other compact auto-loaders. When this type of holster is used it is important to plan how to reach it since it will normally be worn beneath a uniform shirt. Many who use this type of holster, or some of the shoulder holsters discussed in the next section, sew a couple of buttons to the outside of the uniform shirt so it appears unaltered but affix Velcro for purposes of actually closing the shirt.

Fobus Paddle Holster for the Glock 23.

Current military holsters often use ballistic nylon as in the case of this US military holster from Bianchi.

This allows fast access to the back-up weapon by just thrusting the hand through the shirt opening.

The shoulder holster has several appealing characteristics. For example, it is one of the best methods of carrying a heavy weapon. Additionally, under the arm opposite the holster, spare magazine, spare speed-loaders, handcuffs and other gear can be carried. The shoulder holster may also be worn with beltless trousers, shorts and other clothing that does not lend itself to other types of holsters. Many women, in fact, find that shoulder holsters are more comfortable than hip holsters because of their shape. The shoulder holster also allows ease of access with the weak hand as well as the strong one, allowing a draw if the normal shooting hand has been injured.

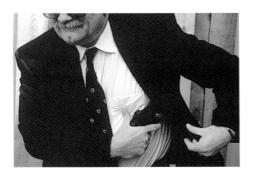

The shoulder holster allows a large weapon to be carried away from the belt. Using the weak hand to help clear the coat during the draw will usually speed up presentation of the weapon.

Although often thought of as intended for carrying a concealed weapon, the shoulder holster is also popular with military personnel, especially armoured crewmen, helicopter pilots and others who will be seated much of the time. Shoulder holsters normally carry the weapon in one of three positions – vertical, slanting downwards or upside down. Each has its own advantages, though the author finds the easiest draws are from the latter two. Vertical shoulder holsters are normally the best for longer-barrelled weapons which are likely to show the outline of the muzzle against the back of the jacket if using a down-slanting rig.

Most good holster makers offer shoulder rigs. The author has most frequently used those from Mitch Rosen, Galco (including the Miami Classic made famous by the *Miami Vice* television series) and Horseshoe Leather. However, other excellent examples of traditional shoulder holsters are available from Bianchi, Don Hume, Kramer, Ted Blocker, De Santis and Gould and Goodrich. Ken Null's City Slicker offers an interesting variation on the upside down rig. Using lightweight plastics, Null has created a rig that is comfortable, light and from which you draw very quickly. It is especially useful for the latest generation of Smith & Wesson scandium .357 Magnum J-frame revolvers. Two makers also offer especially well designed nylon shoulder rigs. Eagle Industries offers shoulder holsters designed for concealment but

The shoulder holster allows a draw with the weak hand in an emergency.

also for military and police special operations personnel who will wear their weapon exposed but want a shoulder rig to get it off of the hip. Uncle Mike's uses a laminate material for the Pro-Pak line of shoulder holsters and are among the most comfortable the author has ever tried.

Many makers of shoulder holsters design their rigs to be modular so that the user can choose how it is set up. For example, instead of a spare magazine pouch under the arm opposite the holster, two holsters can be used. By carrying two examples of the same weapon, it is possible to instantly change to the back-up handgun of the same type should an unclearable malfunction occur in the first weapon. The author uses such double rigs from Horseshoe Leather and Mitch Rosen and is very happy with them.

Fobus belt holster for a Kimber 4in auto pistol.

There are other types of holster, including crotch holsters, suspender holsters and holsters designed to be completely concealed beneath the shirt and trousers. A variation on the latter is what is generally known as the bellyband holster. This type of holster is designed to hold the weapon close to the body underneath a relatively loose shirt. Early US Air Marshals used this method to carry a compact .38 Special revolver. It has also been very popular with undercover police officers. Among makers who offer this type of holster today are Uncle Mike's, De Santis and Gould and Goodrich. The author has successfully used the bellyband holster to conceal small handguns and medium auto-loaders. As with many concealment holsters today, concealment of the Glock

Bianchi nylon holster offers a secure way to carry this Taurus titanium .44 Special revolver.

26 and Glock 27 is often the standard by which such rigs are judged and the bellyband holster will carry these weapons well. The author has always found this type of holster much more comfortable in the winter but somewhat less comfortable in hot weather. Of course, you would mostly use this method of carrying a handgun when wearing light clothing.

A comfortable alternative to the bellyband in hot weather is Kramer Handgun Leather's Confident Shoulder Holster. Fabricated of breathable polyester mesh, the Confident is worn as an undershirt beneath a standard shirt. With a built-in holster under each arm, the Confident allows you to carry a handgun on the side best for you or to carry two guns. Although the author has carried the Glock 27 in the Confident, it would work especially well with today's titanium and scandium revolvers.

A popular method of carrying a handgun as well as badge, handcuffs, ASP baton and other gear is in what in the USA is called the 'fanny-pack' holster. Designed to look like the bumbags worn by joggers, hikers, bikers and other sports people, this holster can comfortably carry even a relatively large handgun. Many of the major holster manufacturers offer fanny-pack holsters including Galco, De Santis, Uncle Mike's

and Bianchi. These holsters are very popular with law enforcement and military special operations personnel who may have to be armed while wearing very casual clothing. US Department of State Security Special Agents are especially fond of this method of carrying a weapon.

Ken Null is one of the few US makers who offers a holster for the Korth revolver.

Galco offers finely crafted briefcases and handbags designed for carrying a concealed handgun.

The best-designed fanny-pack holsters often incorporate a 'tear away' feature which allows very fast access to the weapon in an emergency. Variations which resemble mobile-phone carriers or even pager carriers are also available for carrying smaller weapons. To make it less obvious that the bumbag is actually a holster for a handgun, some manufacturers use softer colours. De Santis, for example, offers its 'Gunny Sacks' in black, green, blue or burgundy, while Galco offers its line in very high quality leather.

Some manufacturers even offer clothing with a holster built in. One such company, Concealed Carry Clothiers (CCC), offers a line of nicely made vests which incorporate pockets with specially fitted holsters to carry an assortment of handguns. The author frequently uses a denim CCC vest; it is a comfortable way to carry to second gun while concealing the one he has on his belt.

Although most who carry a handgun do not like the idea of it being kept in a carrier separate from their person, some do use briefcases, handbags and oversized male wallets designed to conceal a handgun. These have the disadvantage, however, of allowing someone to snatch the carrier, thus gaining control of the weapon. Galco offers an especially handsome line of handbags to carry a handgun as well as attractive and functional briefcases with a holster built in. The author has used one of Galco's briefcases to carry a large

Concealed Carry Clothiers vest illustrating the draw from a side pocket. (CCC)

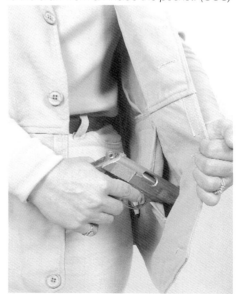

Concealed Carry Clothiers vest designed to carry a handgun in various ways. Illustrated is the draw from an inside the pocket. (CCC)

handgun, while carrying a more compact weapon on his person. Galco also offers a backpack purse with a built-in holster as does Bianchi. De Santis offers a more functional handbag with built-in holster specifically designed for female police officers. Mitch Rosen's family has a long history in the handbag business so it is no surprise that his Portfolio Case is a handsome, utilitarian method for carrying both papers and a weapon. Note, too, that some briefcases designed for law enforcement personnel in which to carry their weapons also have a built-in Kevlar panel allowing them to be used as bullet shields.

Certainly this chapter has not covered every type of holster that has been used nor has it covered other methods of carrying a handgun. It is an overview of the best, in the view of the author, in contemporary combat holsters.

Military issue holster for the Russian PSM pistol.

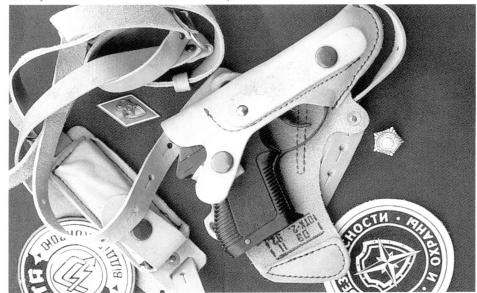

Recommended suppliers of combat holsters

Aker International	**Bianchi International**	**Concealed Carry Clothiers**
2248 Main Street, Suite 6	27969 Jefferson Avenue	PO Box 237
Chula Vista	Temecula	Saunderstown
CA 91911-3932	CA 92590	RI 08274-0237
USA	USA	USA
619 423 5182	909 676 5621	888 959 4500
www.akerleather.com	www.bianchi-intl.com	www.concealedcarry.com

Albrecht Kind GmbH AKAH	**Blade-Tech**	**DeSantis Gunhide**
18–20 Hermann-Kind-Strasse	3060 South 96th Street	PO Box 2039
Gummersbach	Tacoma	New Hyde Park
Germany 51617	WA 98409	NY 11040-0701
011 49 2261 705301	USA	USA
www.akah.de	253 581 4347	www.desantisholster.com
	www.blade-tech.com	

Artesania F. Exposito, S.A.	**Ted Blocker Holsters Inc.**	**Eagle Industries Unlimited Inc.**
Baviera S/N	9396 South-West Tigard Street	400 Biltmore Drive, Suite 530
La Carolinia	Tigard	Fenton
Jaen	OR 97223	MO 63026
Spain	USA	USA
011 34 953 681444	800 650 9742	636 343 7547
www.artesaniaexposito.com	www.tedblocker.com	www.eagleindustries.com

Bell Charter Oak Inc.	**Bulman Gunleather**	**El Paso Saddlery Company**
PO Box 198	PO Box 361	PO Box 27194
Gilbertsville	Newry	El Paso
NY 13776	PA 16665	TX 79926
USA	USA	USA
607 783 2483	814 696 8615	915 544 2233
www.bellcharteroakholsters.com	www.bulmangunleather.com	www.epsaddlery.com

Fobus USA	**Don Hume Leathergoods Inc.**	**Thad Rybka**
1300 Industrial Hwy, Suite B-3	PO Box 351	134 Havilah Hill Street
Southampton	Miami	Odenville
PA 18966	OK 74355-0351	AL 35120
USA	USA	USA
215 355 2621	800 331 2686	
www.fobusholster.com	www.donhume.com	

Galco International Ltd	**Kramer Handgun Leather**	**Milt Sparks Holsters Inc.**
2019 West Quail Avenue	PO Box 112154	605 East 44th #2
Phoenix	Tacoma	Boise
AZ 85027	WA 98411	ID 83714
USA	USA	USA
800 874 2526	800 510 2666	208 377 5577
www.usgalco.com	www.kramerleather.com	www.miltsparks.com

Gould & Goodrich	**K.L. Null Holsters Ltd**	**Uncle Mike's (Michaels of Oregon)**
709 East McNeil Street	161 School Street North-West	PO Box 1690
Lillington	Hill City Station, Resaca	Oregon City
NC 27546	GA 30735	OR 97045
USA	USA	USA
910 893 2071	706 625 5643	503 655 7964
www.gouldusa.com	www.klnullholsters.com	www.michaels-oregon.com

Horseshoe Leather Products	**Mitch Rosen Extraordinary Gunleather**	**Wild Bill's Concealment Holsters**
The Cottage	300 Bedford Street	PO Box 1941
Sharow	Manchester	Garner
Ripon	NH 03101-1102	NC 27529
HG4 5BP	USA	USA
01765 605858	603 647 2971	www.billsconcealment.com
www.horseshoe.co.uk	www.mitchrosen.com	

Chapter 5 **Combat Ammunition**

Any firearm is only as effective as its ammunition and this is especially true of the handgun which is often chosen because of its concealability. In the past, handgun effectiveness was normally predicated on large bores throwing heavy bullets. During the era of percussion weapons, round balls were often chosen for ease of loading but were also often cast of soft lead which would flatten on impact. The earliest cartridge handguns were generally chambered for small-bore rimfire cartridges which lacked stopping power but later centrefire military-cartridge revolvers used heavy, large-

Federal's Personal Defense ammo is specifically designed for home owners who keep a defensive handgun and offers lower recoil with good stopping power. (Federal)

calibre bullets to increase the likelihood of dropping an enemy. The .455 Eley round, for example, was used for decades in Webley revolvers. Its 265-grain rather elongated bullet was known to be much more devastating on tissue than its slow muzzle velocity would indicate. This was achieved through its tendency to tumble once it hit flesh, thus increasing the shock effect. The US .45 Colt calibre also used a heavy bullet though at substantially higher velocity than the .455 Eley.

Other attempts were made during the late nineteenth and early twentieth centuries to increase the effectiveness of combat ammunition. Expanding bullets

Federal's Hydra-Shok loads are among the best for consistent stopping power.

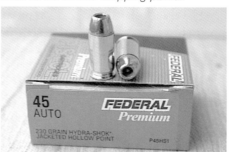

developed at the Dum Dum arsenal in India and used at the Battle of Omdurman have even become a generic term for expanding bullets. Other solutions included the Hoxie bullet which had a hollow cavity containing a ball bearing which, when forced into the cavity, helped the bullet to expand. Blunt 'manstopper' loads for the .455 and .450 Webley cartridges were another attempt

Federal's Hydra-Shok bullet is designed to deliver assured expansion at different ranges.

at creating a cartridge that had greater terminal effect. Such loads were often duplicated on a 'field expedient' basis by reversing round-nosed bullets in their cartridge cases so that the flat base became the striking surface.

The introduction of cleaner smokeless powder late in the nineteenth century allowed the development of the automatic-pistol cartridge. Many of the earliest rounds for the new self-loading pistols relied upon small bullets fired at high velocity. However, since to enhance the functioning of the automatic's action these bullets often had full metal jackets, they tended to be too powerful and passed straight through the target (over-penetration) and were, thus, not noted for

their stopping power. Large bullets for automatic pistols such as those of the US .45 Colt auto or the British .455 Webley auto retained substantial stopping power because of the bullet's weight but most other autos required very precise shot placement to stop an attacker.

Another approach was often taken by American lawmen in the West during the first decades of the twentieth century. While the standard factory loads for many revolvers were somewhat anaemic, by hand loading them with semi-wadcutter bullets very effective manstopping rounds could be created for the .38 Special, .44 Special and .45 Colt.

Although various hollow-pointed bullets had been developed and loaded

No matter how good the ammunition, the shooter must have the ability to place the bullets in the right place.

in the past, it was the introduction of the Super Vel line of cartridges in the 1960s that heralded the modern age of effective combat ammunition. Employing relatively light hollow-cavity bullets at high velocity, Super Vel offered ammunition which effectively expanded and delivered enhanced stopping power against human adversaries. Other specialised loads followed, including the Glaser Safety Slug which employed a projectile comprised of small shot in a liquid Teflon bonding medium. Designed to deliver all of its energy in the target, the Glaser Safety Slug proved very effective. Both Super Vel and Glaser rounds attempted to address the problem of offering a round that would feed effectively through auto-loading pistols yet would expand reliably. Another approach was the German Blitz

Two loads intended for use by law enforcement agencies: above, the Federal 115-grain +P+; below, the Winchester Subsonic 147-grain load.

Glaser Safety Slugs are the best known of the frangible loads designed to deliver energy in the target without over-penetrating.

Action Trauma (BAT) round which employed a light hollow-cavity bullet with a polymer plug that gave it the profile of a round-nosed bullet while in the weapon but upon leaving the barrel the plug was shed leaving a very effective expandable bullet.

A wider array of effective combat ammunition than at any time in history is currently available in various calibres and designed for various missions. In discussing some of these contemporary loads, their effectiveness will be gauged according to their successful 'street stops' or 'street stopping power'. The percentages cited are based on the work of Evan Marshall and are documented in the books on stopping power he has co-authored with Ed Sanow. These statistics were assembled from thousands of

Cor-Bon's Pow'RBall ammo is designed to feed reliably, to penetrate the target and deliver stopping power.

shootings, the information having been forwarded to the authors by coroners, forensic examiners and homicide detectives.

It must be understood, too, that the optimum ammunition for use by an air marshal, who wants to stop a hijacker with the minimum danger of over-penetration, and a high-risk warrant team member who may face a drug dealer wearing a ballistic vest will not be the same. Ammunition can be designed for extreme penetration, extreme expansion or a compromise between the two. Because law enforcement personnel and others outside the USA who are armed but often not permitted to use hollow-point ammunition, there have also been attempts to produce non-hollow-point ammunition that is still effective at

Mag Tech ammo ranks among the best in many calibres.

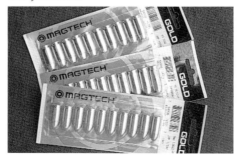

stopping an attacker. The German Blitz Action Trauma round, the French THV, Cor-Bon's Pow'RBall and new loads from Federal all attempt to address this concern.

For ease of reference the most widely used calibres in combat handguns are discussed below with reference to special characteristics of ammunition in that calibre.

.22 LR
As anyone who has worked as a homicide detective or an emergency room surgeon in a large urban American hospital can attest, a large number of people die each year from .22 rimfire wounds. In fact, the .22 has always had a reputation as a killer because its outside-lubricated bullet picks up all sorts of debris which it deposits in a wound, thus increasing the likelihood of infection. The .22 long rifle round is not, however, known for its stopping power. It may kill someone hours or days later but it will only stop their hostile activity if a round is carefully placed, usually into the cranium. Even a head shot is not certain as it is not uncommon for a .22 bullet to hit the skull without penetrating, then follow the curvature around and exit on the other side of the skull.

Nevertheless, the .22 long rifle is used in various derringers and some small auto-loading pistols, including the Walther TPH and Beretta Model 21. In general, an important consideration in choosing a .22 long rifle load for any of these small auto-loaders is finding one that will work reliably, as the relatively long cartridge and the short slide travel often lead to malfunctions. With the two pistols mentioned above the author has had good luck with CCI Stingers and tends to use them when available. Stingers also have some of the best one-shot results on the street but are still only successful about 38 per cent of the time. The .22 long rifle round is an excellent round for practice but is certainly not an effective choice for combat.

5.7×28 Cartridge

Developed originally by FN for the P90 submachine gun, the 5.7mm round is also used in the FN Five-seveN® pistols which will be discussed later in this book. Intended to replace the 9×19 round as a military cartridge, in its SS190 configuration, the 5.7×28 uses a 31-grain jacketed bullet with a penetrator at a muzzle velocity of 2346ft/sec. Based on the assumption that the soldier on today's battlefield will be facing an enemy wearing a ballistic vest and helmet, the 5.7×28 round is designed to penetrate body armour, yet remain in the body of a human target. It shoots very flat, allowing its user to engage a target more

effectively at longer range. The SS190 round will, in fact, defeat Threat Level III-A body armour at 200yd.

5.45×18 Russian

Developed for the Soviet (Russian) PSM pistol, the 5.45×18 round allowed the pistol to be designed with a very slim line. Although it will not penetrate as many layers of Kevlar as the 5.7×28 round, it has better penetration than virtually any other standard handgun cartridge.

.25 ACP

Although this tiny pistol cartridge has been around since 1908 and remains popular today, it is not really very effective. Its rate of one-shot stops on the street runs at around 25 per cent.

Two loads designed to punch through body armour: left, the French THV; right, the FN 5.7mm.

However, so many small automatic pistols have been chambered for this cartridge over the years that it remains very popular, especially as a 'lady's' gun or a hideout gun for undercover police officers and others. It has also been carried by high-ranking military officers, more as a badge of authority than as a practical combat weapon. Normally, the standard 50-grain full metal jacket ammunition is used in this calibre but Glaser does offer a 35-grain Safety Slug load at 1150ft/sec.

.30 Mauser/7.62×25 Tokarev

Although the .30 Mauser round has normally been loaded slightly lighter than the Tokarev round, the two are virtually interchangeable. Because of the ubiquity of the TT-30 and TT-33 Tokarev pistols as well as the Czech M52 pistol in many parts of the world, this remains a widely distributed combat handgun cartridge. An infamous user of this calibre was Carlos 'The Jackal' who employed a CZ 52 in a shootout with French security forces. Prior to the introduction of the 5.7×28 and 5.45×18 rounds, the 7.62×25 had the reputation of being the best penetrative round of standard handgun cartridges against body armour.

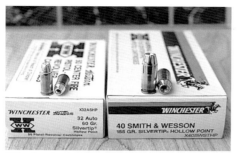

Winchester's Silvertip hollow-point loads are among the most popular for combat. The Silvertip .32 ACP load has been widely used in pocket pistols.

.32 ACP

Once very popular in Europe as a police and even as a military round, the .32 ACP has now decreased in popularity as most of those needing a combat handgun have opted for something more powerful. The combination of a large number of high-quality surplus automatics in this calibre such as the Walther PP and PPK and the availability of very small auto-loaders such as the Seecamp and the Autauga in this calibre has prompted manufacturers to offer a variety of loads in this calibre.

Although the traditional 71-grain jacketed hollow-point bullet will function most reliably through older .32 auto-loaders, modern loads such as the

Winchester Silvertip and the Federal Hydra-Shok offer more stopping power; 66 per cent of one-shot stops on the street for the Silvertip. Other loads designed to increase stopping power in .32 ACP include the Glaser Safety Slug, MagSafe Defender and Triton Quick-Shok. The 55-grain Glaser Safety Slug at 1300ft/sec is the favourite of some undercover police officers who carry a .32 auto as their hideout gun.

.380 ACP

The .380, also known as the 9×17, 9mm Kurz and 9mm Corto, is generally the minimum that is considered acceptable for combat and only marginally so at that. The advantage of the .380 round is that a substantial number of compact, high-quality auto-loading pistols are chambered for it. The Walther PPK and Star DK are the author's personal favourites in this calibre but numerous other acceptable weapons are available in this calibre.

The two best combat loads based on street results are Federal's Hydra-Shok and Cor-Bon's jacketed hollow-point (JHP), both running at 71 per cent. Triton's Quick-Shok with 70 per cent one-shot stops and Winchester's Silvertip with 68 per cent one-shot stops have also proved effective. The Magtech 85-grain JHP produces a muzzle velocity of

1080ft/sec and employs a bullet designed for expansion. The author also likes the Glaser Silver Tip 70-grain Safety Slug load in this calibre.

9mm Makarov (9×18)

The standard handgun cartridge in the Warsaw Pact and Third World countries within the Soviet sphere of influence for decades, the 9mm Makarov is more powerful than the .380 but less powerful than the 9×19 in its standard loading. However, a heavier Makarov load, designated for 'high penetration' and designed for the later delayed blowback PMM Makarov, has ballistics similar to the 9×19 (9mm Parabellum) round. Although this load and special frangible loads are available to Russian police and military units, it was not until the Makarov pistol was imported into the USA in substantial quantity that really effective loads were developed.

The three combat loads the author has found to be accurate and reliable in 9mm Makarov pistols are the MagSafe 51-grain Defender load, the CCI-Speer 90-grain Gold Dot and the Cor-Bon 95-grain JHP. Any of these should offer stopping power somewhat better than the .380 loads discussed above.

9mm Parabellum (9×19)

Probably the most popular combat handgun cartridge in the world, the 9×19 is available in a myriad of loadings. Federal's 115-grain JHP +P+ load has traditionally proved to be the most effective in this calibre with one-shot stop rates over 90 per cent. The +P+ designates that these loads are of higher than standard velocity and sales are usually limited to law enforcement and military agencies. Other +P+ loadings from Winchester and Remington, as well as Federal's 124-grain Hydra-Shok +P+, CCI-Speer's 124-grain Gold Dot and Cor-Bon's 115-grain JHP, all have street stop rates in the 88–9 per cent range. Although not involved in enough street shootings to be rated, Magtech's 115-grain JHP has a good reputation for expansion as well.

Federal's 115-grain +P+ load, one of the best 9mm combat rounds.

The author also likes the BeeSafe, the Glaser 80-grain Safety Slug and the MagSafe Stealth load, all of which use frangible bullets which are designed to dump the maximum amount of energy in the target. He also thinks highly of the Black Hills 115-grain JHP load. Black Hills does a lot of loading for military and police units and produces consistently high quality ammunition. Along with Federal's 115-grain +P+ and Cor-Bon's 115-grain JHP, this Black Hills load is the best choice for precision shot placement. There are other highly accurate 9mm loads but these three are consistently accurate with a wide variety of 9mm pistols.

.38 Super

Originally developed in 1929 to give law officers a round capable of engaging heavily armed criminals in vehicles, the .38 Super round has undergone a resurgence during the last decade. Two manufacturers offer very effective loads in this calibre: Cor-Bon offers 115-grain and 125-grain jacketed hollow-point loads, while Winchester offers a 125-grain Silvertip load. Any of these three loads offers ballistics superior to the 9×19.

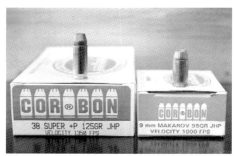

Two Cor-Bon combat loads for the .38 Super and the 9mm Makarov.

.357 SIG

Based on a necked-down .40 S&W case, the .357 SIG round has gained respect with its adoption by two high-profile US federal agencies, the Secret Service and the FAA Air Marshals. It has been suggested that the genesis for this round was the desire by law enforcement agencies for a round similar to the cartridge they were using in .357 Magnum revolvers. However, to achieve its high velocity, the .357 SIG round operates at up to 40,000 pounds per square inch (psi) of pressure, ranking it as the highest pressure round normally used for combat handguns.

The .357 SIG's results on the street have been impressive. Federal's 125-grain JHP has a rate of 92 per cent in actual shootings, while Cor-Bon's

Black Hills .357 SIG 125-grain JHP, one of the most powerful automatic pistol loads.

125-grain JHP, CCI-Speer's 125-grain Gold Dot, Federal's 125-grain Tactical and Cor-Bon's 125-grain JHP are all very close at over 90 per cent. MagSafe's 64-grain Defender and BeeSafe's 91-grain offer excellent frangible loads.

.38 Special
For much of the twentieth century, the .38 Special was the standard police cartridge in the USA and in many other parts of the world. It has also seen substantial military use. Although it has been superseded as a primary combat round in many cases, it remains popular among uniformed private security personnel in the USA. In snub, compact revolvers, the .38 Special also remains a widely used cartridge. In fact, the round is so popular in 2in barrelled revolvers that Marshall and Sanow tabulate street stopping power results for this barrel length as well as the 4in.

From 2in barrelled guns, the three best loads successfully stop attackers with one shot about two-thirds of the time. Federal has three loads that have done well from the short barrel: the 158-grain lead hollow-point (LHP) +P, the 129-grain Hydra-Shok +P (one of the author's own favourites from snub revolvers) and the 125-grain JHP +P. From 4in barrelled guns, the loads with the best stopping power run at around 80 per cent in one-shot stops with Winchester's 110-grain JHP +P+ coming out top. As with most +P+ loads, this one was developed for use by law enforcement agencies. One of the author's favourites, Cor-Bon's 115-grain JHP +P, has a street stop rate of 79 per cent. Federal's 158-grain LHP+P comes in at 76 per cent.

The .38 Special is a very accurate load and some of the loads mentioned already are also known for their accuracy, including the Federal loads and Cor-Bon's 115-grain JHP+P. The Black Hills 125-grain JHP is another very accurate load. A couple of other loads are worthy of note. Federal's 110-grain Hydra-Shok Personal Defence round is designed for mild recoil and good expansion. As the name implies, this ammunition was designed specifically for those who carry a .38 Special or keep one around the home or business for self-defence.

.357 Magnum
Developed in 1935 as the 'world's most powerful handgun cartridge', the .357 Magnum no longer retains that distinction but it remains a very effective combat round. In fact, the highest rate of one-shot stops in street shootings has consistently been with the Federal and Remington 125-grain JHP loads which are currently running at 96 per cent. CCI's, Black Hills's and Cor-Bon's 125-grain JHP loads are close behind. Any of these five loads should give great confidence in a revolver so loaded.

Expanded Federal Hydra-Shok bullet. (Federal)

However, to be effective, any bullet must be placed well by the shooter. Note also that the .357 Magnum round can be very accurate.

The .357 Magnum has gained new popularity with the availability of the very light, compact .357 Smith & Wesson scandium revolvers. Note that these guns are not recommended for use with the light 110-grain .357 Magnum JHP loads which are more likely to erode the forcing cone. This combination offers perhaps the best trade-off between power and ease of carry of any modern combat handgun.

Although the 125-grain JHP .357 Magnum loads have performed well from short-barrelled guns as well as from 4in barrels, some who carry a .357 Magnum snub-nose like loads which use a heavier bullet and do not depend so much on

Expanded CCI-Speer Gold Dot bullet. (CCI-Speer)

velocity. The Federal 158-grain Hydra-Shok and the Cor-Bon 140-grain JHP are especially popular with those who prefer the heavier bullets. The 91-grain BeeSafe round at 1525ft/sec is rated at 90 per cent in one-shot stops for those who may need a frangible load, i.e. air or sea marshals, nuclear security or others who might have to shoot where over-penetration or ricochet could be a danger. The author also likes both the Glaser Blue Tip (which uses #12 shot) and the Silver Tip (which uses #6 shot) loads, both safety slugs weighing 80 grains and firing at 1800ft/sec.

.40 Smith & Wesson
The .40 S&W round has become extremely popular with many US law enforcement agencies, being the current issue cartridge with the FBI among other agencies. It has also achieved some acceptance with law enforcement agencies in other parts of the world. In countries which forbid civilian use of 'military' calibres, thus restricting the use of 9×19 and .45 ACP, the .40 S&W has offered a powerful alternative. In fact, the .40 S&W was, to some extent, developed to combine appealing features of the 9×19 and .45 ACP cartridges.

For those who like larger bullets, the .40 offers a 180-grain JHP load, while for those who like the large magazine

capacity of the 9×19, the .40 S&W usually can be used in a double-column magazine. In fact, most guns designed for the 9×19 round can also be chambered for the .40 S&W with a few modifications. The best combat loads for the .40 S&W are now running at well over 90 per cent in one-shot stops, with the Remington 165-grain Golden Saber having a slight edge at 94 per cent, closely followed by Federal's 155-grain Hydra-Shok and CCI's 155-grain Gold Dot loads, each at 93 per cent. Federal's 155-grain JHP and Cor-Bon's 135-grain JHP are both rated at 89 per cent, closely followed by Cor-Bon's 150-grain JHP and Federal's 180-grain Hydra-Shok, each at 88 per cent.

Federal's 180-grain Hydra-Shok has the best rating of the heavier .40 S&W bullets. The Black Hills 180-grain JHP and Cor-Bon's 180-grain JHP, both very accurate loads, rank at 84 per cent and 86 per cent respectively. Another load worthy of note is Magtech's 155-grain JHP which produces a muzzle velocity of 1205ft/sec and is known for excellent expansion. As with other popular combat calibres, Federal offers their Personal Defence Ammo in .40 S&W, in this case a 135-grain Hydra-Shok load. The BeeSafe is an excellent choice in frangible ammunition, being loaded with a 101-grain bullet with a muzzle velocity of 1350ft/sec for a street one-shot stop rating of 86 per cent.

10mm

The 10mm round actually preceded the .40 S&W, both of which use the same bullets. The FBI's adoption of the 10mm round initially seemed to herald a great future but the .40 S&W achieved far greater success. Even the FBI replaced the 10mm with the .40 S&W. The 10mm round is available in two loadings, one medium and one heavy. The heavy load makes the 10mm the most powerful auto normally used as a service weapon. The 10mm round is also very accurate.

Three of the top five rounds in street stops are from Federal: the 155-grain JHP at 89 per cent and the 180-grain Hydra-Shok and 180-grain JHP, both at 85 per cent. Cor-Bon's 150-grain JHP leads in one-shot stops at 90 per cent.

Two Cor-Bon loads which deliver excellent stopping power: the 10mm auto and .44 Special.

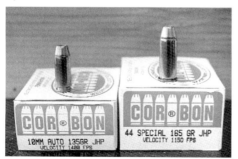

The author has shot a reasonable amount with each of these four loads and has found them all to be very accurate.

.41 Magnum

The .41 Magnum occupies a position among revolver rounds somewhat analogous to the 10mm round among autos. It was originally designed to give those in law enforcement a round more powerful than the .357 Magnum yet with less recoil than the .44 Magnum. The author has always had special affection for this cartridge since he carried a Model 58 Smith & Wesson .41 Magnum as a young deputy sheriff. The .41 Magnum has traditionally been loaded with a 210-grain lead bullet with a medium muzzle velocity and a 210-grain jacketed soft-point or jacketed hollow-point at high velocity.

In street shootings, Winchester's 170-grain Silvertip scored 90 per cent one-shot stops. Although not enough street results were available on two other loads which the author likes, he believes that they will perform as well or better. Federal's 210-grain Hi-Shok hollow-point load and Cor-Bon's 170-grain JHP load are also excellent choices in this calibre. In shootings using the lighter lead SWC loads, one-shot stops ran at about 75 per cent.

Cor-Bon's 165-grain .45 ACP load delivers devastating stopping power.

.44 Special

For much of the twentieth century, the .44 Special cartridge was popular with Western lawmen but, to really maximise it, it was necessary to hand load. Only within the last twenty years or so have really good combat loads been available commercially for the .44 Special. An interesting transition has taken place, too, in the weapons for this calibre. While large-frame Smith & Wesson revolvers were the primary arms used in this calibre for decades, the trend over the last thirty years has been for more compact and lightweight weapons such as the Charter Arms Bulldog, the Smith & Wesson Models 296 and 396 and the Taurus Model 445T.

The best street results for the .44 Special have been obtained with Winchester's 200-grain Silvertip at 75 per cent. Federal's 200-grain lead semi-wadcutter hollow-point did almost as well. There are, however, other rounds available which are as effective or more effective than these but they have not been involved in enough shootings to have been tallied in the stopping-power surveys carried out by Marshall and Sanow. Cor-Bon's 165-grain JHP load is very accurate and at 1150ft/sec should expand quite well. This load is also especially well suited for the titanium Smith & Wesson and Taurus .44 Special revolvers as the lighter bullet is less likely to jump the crimp under recoil. Glaser's 135-grain Safety Slug in both configurations and MagSafe's 92-grain Defender and 115-grain Urban Defence offer excellent choices in frangible ammunition.

The Black Hills .44 Magnum 300-grain JHP offers excellent stopping power against man or beast.

.44 Magnum

Although there are now specialised handgun cartridges designed for hunters which are more powerful, the .44 Magnum remains the most powerful handgun cartridge likely to be used for combat. At least partially as a result of the Clint Eastwood series of Dirty Harry films which featured a San Francisco detective who carried a Smith & Wesson Model 29 .44 Magnum, there have been a reasonable number of police officers who have used this calibre, though it has never really been a popular combat round. Today, the best justification for this calibre would be for those who work in areas where they might have to defend themselves against four-footed as well as two-footed 'beasts.' In Alaska, for example, a substantial number of residents carry a .44 Magnum revolver to deal with either bears or criminals.

Ironically, despite the .44 Magnum's great power, it has never ranked among the best handgun cartridges in street stopping power. This may well be because this round generates such substantial recoil that many who use it cannot really place their shots effectively. Even the best load, Winchester's 210-grain Silvertip, only results in one-shot stops about 92 per cent of the time. Others which rank high are Federal's 180-grain JHP and 240-grain Hydra-Shok. Another load which the author especially likes is the Black Hills 300-grain JHP load which offers a heavy bullet load for use against man or beast. The best choice for the .44 Magnum for anti-personnel combat may well be the Glaser 135-grain Safety Slug at 1850ft/sec as this frangible projectile will deliver the .44 Magnum's devastating power without the over-penetration likely to occur with many other loads in this calibre.

.45 ACP

In the days when automatic pistol ammunition was loaded almost entirely with full-jacketed bullets designed to feed reliably, aficionados of the .45 ACP used to say 'They all fall to hardball!'. The

Cor-Bon's .45 ACP 165-grain jacketed hollow-point is known to be an excellent stopper. The wound cavity from this cartridge is illustrated here in ballistic gelatin. (Cor-Bon)

One of the author's favourite combat handgun cartridges is the .41 Magnum. Illustrated are two of the best loads in this calibre.

implication was that the 230-grain full-metal cased military .45 ACP round was a sure stopper. Compared to full-metal jacketed 9mm rounds, it certainly was better but the FMC .45 ACP load has been far surpassed by the best of today's combat loads. In fact, Federal's 230-grain Hydra-Shok and Remington's 185-grain Golden Saber have a remarkable 96 per cent one-shot stop rate in shootings. CCI's Gold Dot, sometimes termed the 'flying ash tray' because of its massive hollow cavity, is close behind with 93 per cent. Cor-Bon's 185-grain also has a quite satisfactory 90 per cent one-shot stop rate and the author has been informed by reliable sources that the Cor-Bon 165-grain JHP has performed as

well or better. The author also likes the Black Hills 230-grain JHP +P load which is very accurate as well as having ballistics similar to the top two stoppers.

Recently, he has been experimenting with Magtech's 185-grain JHP which produces a muzzle velocity of 1150ft/sec and has a reputation for excellent expansion. Once again, Glaser with a 145-grain Safety Slug at 1350ft/sec and MagSafe with four different loads are the best of the frangible loads. Just as a point of interest, the 230-grain hard-ball round mentioned at the beginning of this section shows one-shot street stops of about 62 per cent.

.45 Colt

Much as the .45 ACP had been the dominant automatic pistol round prior to the ready availability of modern expanding bullets, the .45 Colt with its large, blunt 255-grain bullet had retained its reputation for stopping power since its introduction in 1873 for the Colt Single Action Army Revolver. Among more modern ammunition, Federal's 225-grain SWHP and Winchester's 225-grain Silvertip both have one-shot stop rates of about 80 per cent. Glaser and MagSafe both offer frangible loads for the .45 Colt as well.

The Black Hills .45 ACP 230-grain JHP is very accurate as well as a good manstopper.

The .45 Colt round is still considered a good stopper because of its heavy bullet. Federal's 225-grain SWHP is one of the better combat loads for this calibre.

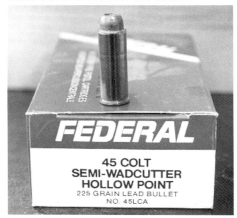

DIRECTORY

Glock 17 **Austria**

The Glock 17 was the first of this innovative line of pistols and remains one of the most popular. The Glock's polymer frame, which was controversial at its time of introduction, has now proved to be both durable and light and has helped make the Glock one of the world's most popular combat pistols. The fast-action trigger allows the Glock to be carried ready for instant action by a pull on the trigger which contains a small internal lever safety but no external safeties have to be released. Trigger pull may be easily adjusted by switching out the trigger bar or sear but a 5lb pull is usually considered standard. The latest generation full-sized and compact Glocks come equipped with a built-in rail for lasers or lights. The full-sized service Glock is available in .40 S&W as the Model 22 and in .357 SIG as the Model 31. Note that the Glock 17 is produced in a special sub-aqua version designed for combat swimmers to fire under water.

Calibre 9mm
Type Fast-action semi-auto
Overall length 7.3in
Barrel length 4.5in
Weight 22oz
Sights Front post, rear square notch, white dot and outline or tritium night sights
Cartridge capacity 17+1 rounds

Glock 18 Austria

The selective-fire Glock 18 is one of only two true machine pistols currently produced in any quantity. With a cyclic rate of 1200rds/min, this is a difficult pistol to control. However, the polymer frame does cushion recoil and make it easier to hold on target at close range than most selective-fire pistols. Unlike most other selective-fire pistols, the Glock 18 does not come with a shoulder stock but is an optional accessory. This and the fact that the Glock 18 is virtually identical externally to the Glock 17 except for a selector switch located on the slide allows this pistol to be carried in standard Glock holsters. The Glock 18 is a highly specialised weapon which will only be used by members of VIP-protection teams or special military or police units. It takes a great deal of practice to attain expertise with it. Therefore, anyone using the Glock 18 must practice constantly to keep the expertise to accurately fire short bursts.

Calibre 9mm
Type Selective-fire machine pistol
Overall length 7.3in
Barrel length 4.5in
Weight 22oz
Sights Front post, rear square notch
Cartridge capacity 17, 19 and
   33+1 rounds

When loaded with full-power 10mm loads, this is the most powerful Glock pistol and, thus, has proved to be popular with rural law officers who might have to dispatch an injured large animal as well as deal with lawbreakers. Many also find this to be one of the most accurate Glock pistols due to the inherent accuracy of the cartridge. To handle the more powerful chambering, this is a somewhat heftier design than the Glock 17. The Model 21 is virtually identical to the Model 20 but is chambered for the .45 ACP round. Also available are the Model 29, a compact version of the Model 20, and the Model 30, a compact version of the Model 21.

Glock 20 (T.J. Mullin)

Calibre 10mm
Type Fast-action semi-auto
Overall length 7.6in
Barrel length 4.6in
Weight 26.3oz
Sights Front post, rear square notch, white dot and outline or tritium night sights
Cartridge capacity 13+1 rounds

Glock 27   Austria

This sub-compact Glock, along with its siblings, the Glock 26 in 9mm and the Glock 33 in .357 SIG, is designed to offer a very compact, hideout, full-powered pistol. An armourer who works on a lot of Glocks once told the author that the compact Glocks actually outsold the full-sized Glock in some areas. They are very popular with law enforcement officers who carry a full-sized Glock as a duty weapon. The smaller Glock may be carried off duty or as a second gun in a pocket, ankle or ballistic-vest holster. It has the additional advantage of accepting the larger capacity magazine of the full-sized Glocks in the same calibre. The Glock 26, Glock 27 and Glock 33 rank among the best of the very compact pistols chambered for a true service cartridge.

Calibre .40 S&W
Type Fast-action semi-auto
Overall length 6.3in
Barrel length 3.5in
Weight 19.8oz
Sights Front post, rear square notch, white dot and outline or tritium night sights
Cartridge capacity 9+1 rounds

Glock 32　　　　　　　　　　　　　　　　**Austria**

This and the other compact Glocks –
the Model 19 in 9mm and the Model 23
in .40 S&W – are the author's
favourites. Daily, he carried one of this
size of Glock for many years and
always found it reliable and comfortable
when carried for long hours. As with the
sub-compact Glocks, the compact
Glocks will take the same magazine as
the full-sized versions in the same
calibre which allows them to use the
higher capacity magazine for reloads.
Although the author has medium-sized
hands, he finds this Glock the most
comfortable to shoot as do many
others. Many law enforcement agencies
which issue the Glock offer their
personnel the choice of the full-sized or
compact model. The NYPD uses the
Glock 19 as a service weapon for both
uniformed personnel and detectives,
an indication of the versatility of this
size of Glock.

Calibre .357 SIG
Type Fast-action semi-auto
Overall length 6.85in
Barrel length 4in
Weight 21.2oz
Sights Front post, rear square notch, white
　　dot and outline or tritium night sights
Cartridge capacity 13+1 rounds

Glock 35

Austria

This Glock and the 9mm version, the Model 34, are sometimes referred to as Practical/Tactical models, indicating that they can be used in practical shooting competitions as well as in true tactical situations. The Model 35 is generally the most accurate of the .40 S&W Glocks, just as the Model 34 is generally the most accurate of the 9mm Glocks. A combination of the slightly longer sight radius, adjustable sights and smooth 3.5lb trigger pull contribute to this accuracy. For combat use, this pistol would have most applications as a second gun for VIP-protection personnel to offer longer-range engagement capability or as the primary weapon for tactical units which might need more precise shot placement on hostage rescue operations.

Above, Glock 22; below, Glock 35; both use the same basic frame (T.J. Mullin)

Calibre .40 S&W
Type Fast-action semi-auto
Overall length 8.15in
Barrel length 5.3in
Weight 24.5oz
Sights Front post, rear adjustable, fixed night sights available
Cartridge capacity 15+1 rounds

The Model M has some very innovative and interesting features. The polymer frame incorporates a grip set at a 111-degree angle to enhance natural pointing. This pistol also utilises the Reset Action Safety System as well as a manual safety which can be released by the trigger finger by pushing up within the trigger guard. An additional safety feature is an integrated limited access lock which comes with two keys. On law enforcement models of the Model M, a handcuff key will work the lock, while a civilian version comes with its own key. Another interesting feature is the sights which incorporate a triangular front sight with a white triangular insert and a trapezoidal rear sight, the latter outlined in white. With practice these sights allow for rapid target acquisition. At the rear of the slide is a loaded chamber indicator which may be seen or felt with the finger as an added safety feature.

Steyr Model M (T.J. Mullin)

Calibre 9mm, .40 S&W and .357 SIG
Type Reset-action semi-auto
Overall length 7.1in
Barrel length 4in
Weight 28oz
Sights Triangle/trapezoid
Cartridge capacity 14+1 rounds (9mm)

FN Five-seveN®

The Five-seveN® is one of the most advanced new military pistols in decades. Designed on the assumption that enemy military personnel encountered on future battlefields will be wearing ballistic armour, the Five-seveN® uses a small, high-velocity bullet intended to penetrate body armour or Kevlar helmets. The flat-shooting cartridge also offers a much flatter trajectory over long range. Another positive feature for a weapon normally carried as a secondary or primary weapon by those with support functions or assigned to aircraft, armoured vehicles or crew-served weapons is that the Five-seveN® is very light. Additionally, it uses a twenty-round magazine which allows forty extra rounds to be easily carried with two spare magazines.

Calibre 5.7×28
Type Fast-action semi-auto
Overall length 8.15in
Barrel length 5.65in
Weight 21.5oz
Sights Front blade, rear notch
Cartridge capacity 20+1 rounds

FN Forty-Nine

The Forty-Nine is designed as a contemporary police or military pistol with a polymer frame and integral rails for lights or lasers. The double-action-only trigger has a pull of about 10lb which is relatively heavy but very consistent and with practice you can shoot quite accurately with this pistol at combat ranges. The Forty-Nine is designed for very safe operation, the firing pin being completely uncocked until the trigger is pulled. Another useful feature is extended, modular slide rails which provide a greater area for contact between the slide and the frame, thus enhancing accuracy. The combination of stainless steel for the barrel and slide and polymer for the frame enhances durability. The Forty-Nine is easily field stripped for maintenance and overall is one of most user-friendly of current combat autos.

Calibre .40 S&W and 9mm
Type Striker-fired, double-action only semi-auto
Overall length 7.75in
Barrel length 4.25in
Weight 26.3oz
Sights Front post, rear square notch, white dot night sight
Cartridge capacity 14+1 rounds (.40 S&W)

FN Hi-Power

Belgium

John Browning's last design, the Hi-Power, has been one of the world's great combat handguns for well over half a century. For much of that time, in fact, it was the most popular combat handgun in the world. The Hi-Power pioneered the double-column, high-capacity magazine for combat pistols, yet retains one of the most comfortable grips of any automatic pistol. The magazine-disconnect safety which renders the pistol inoperable when the magazine is removed is a good safety feature for a pistol used by police and military personnel. In earlier examples of the Hi-Power, the sights were very rudimentary and the safety was so small it was hard to operate. In the latest versions, however, these defects have been fixed, allowing the Hi-Power to remain a premier combat pistol. FN now offers a double-action version of the Hi-Power as well.

Calibre 9mm and .40 S&W
Type Single-action semi-auto
Overall length 7.9in
Barrel length 4.65in
Weight 31oz
Sights Front post, rear square notch
Cartridge capacity 13+1 rounds (9mm)

Rossi Model R462

The Brazilian firm of Rossi manufactures a line of reliable yet inexpensive combat revolvers. In addition to .357 Magnum, Rossi revolvers are also available in .38 Special. Stainless steel and matt blue finishes are available as are 4in and 6in barrels. The availability of Taurus and Smith & Wesson .357 Magnum compact revolvers fabricated of titanium or scandium makes the R462 seem very heavy, so heavy that it is really a belt gun, even with a 2in barrel.

Rossi Model R462 (Rossi)

Calibre .357 Magnum
Type Double-action revolver
Overall length 6.5in
Barrel length 2in
Weight 26oz
Sights Front ramp, rear notch
Cartridge capacity 6 rounds

Taurus Model 85T

Brazil

This UltraLite titanium snub revolver offers a highly concealable, light .38 Special revolver which will safely handle +P loads. There is also a shrouded-hammer version of the Model 85 titanium which is even easier to carry in the pocket since it lacks an exposed hammer to snag on clothing. In fact, it may be fired through a pocket if necessary, though burning powder residue might make the pocket catch fire! The Model 85 does not use the Gripper grips which are standard on the larger titanium revolvers but the finger-grooved rubber grips are quite comfortable. Another useful combat feature is an extended ejector rod which allows full extraction of spent cases. The Model 85 is ported to reduce recoil and muzzle flip. Overall, this is one of the best of the compact .38 Special revolvers currently available.

Calibre .38 Special
Type Double-action revolver
Overall length 6.5in
Barrel length 2in
Weight 13.5oz
Sights Front ramp, rear notch
Cartridge capacity 5 rounds

This big-bore titanium Taurus offers the knock-down power of the .44 Special cartridge but with quite low recoil due to a combination of a ported barrel and the Taurus Ribber grips which do a good job of cushioning. Two versions of the 445 titanium are available, one with a shadow grey finish and the other with a matt spectrum-blue finish. Both are quite handsome yet businesslike. As with other titanium revolvers, the forged titanium barrels are lined, in the case of the .445 with a high-tensile strength stainless bore liner. Although this big-bore combat revolver is still rather large to carry in a pocket, its combination of light weight and low recoil still make it very appealing.

Calibre .44 Special
Type Double-action revolver
Overall length 6. 6in
Barrel length 2in
Weight 19.8oz
Sights Front ramp, rear notch
Cartridge capacity 5 rounds

Taurus Model PT-111Ti Brazil

The PT-111 is most noteworthy for its use of a combination of polymer and titanium to create an especially light 9mm pistol. Even the version with a steel slide only weighs about 3oz more than the standard version. This pistol is also known as the Millennium for its date of introduction. As with other Taurus handguns, the PT-111 is available with a built-in safety key lock. It also incorporates a loaded chamber indicator. All Taurus pistols come with a lifetime warranty as well, an indication of their sturdiness. The author has, in fact, known of Taurus automatic pistols used daily at commercial ranges, firing 100,000 rounds or more without failing.

Taurus Model PT-111Ti (Taurus)

Calibre 9mm
Type Double-action only semi-auto
Overall length 6.1in
Barrel length 3.3in

Weight 15.8oz
Sights Front post, rear combat square notch, night sights
Cartridge capacity 10+1 rounds

Taurus PT-945

This large-calibre, compact semi-auto incorporates one of Taurus's most useful features: the three-position safety. Using this safety, the hammer may be dropped for double-action use or locked back for cocked-and-locked carrying. The PT-945 incorporates other Taurus safety features as well, including the loaded chamber indicator and the key lock. A fancy version is available in blued steel with gold highlights, while a stainless steel version offers even more durability.

Taurus PT-945 (Taurus)

Calibre .45 ACP
Type Double-action semi-auto
Overall length 7.5in
Barrel length 4.3in
Weight 29.5oz
Sights Front post, rear notch, 3-dot
   combat, night sights
Cartridge capacity 8+1 rounds

Para-Ordnance LDA D14 Canada

This is the full-sized, double-action version of the Para-Ordnance pistol. The designation LDA stands for light double-action, good nomenclature for the Para-Ordnance double-action gun which feels more like a self-cocker such as the Daewoo. The consistent double-action pull is very safe yet allows ease of use. The double-actions are available in blued steel or stainless steel. As with the single-action Para-Ordnance pistols, the D14's grip is quite comfortable despite the large magazine capacity. The advantage of carrying the pistol hammer down in double-action will make this Para-Ordnance appeal to many who carry a weapon for duty purposes. The fact that the ambidextrous safety may be applied while the hammer is down is especially appealing in case the pistol gets taken away from its authorised user since a pull on the trigger will not activate the action when the safety is applied.

Calibre .45 ACP
Type Light double-action only semi-auto
Overall length 8.5in
Barrel length 5in
Weight 40oz
Sights Adjustable
Cartridge capacity 14+1 rounds

Although Para-Ordnance established its reputation initially with its high-capacity pistols, this single-stack double-action offers a lot as a concealed-carry weapon. Its short overall length combined with a bobbed hammer and grip safety make it a compact holster gun. Its tritium night sights are another plus for a combat weapon that is normally more likely to be used at night rather than during the day. This pistol is what is often known as the 'Colt Officers Model' size, which means that the Colt takes the same holsters and magazine as this compact pistol. The light double-action which allows this pistol to be carried very safely yet ready for instant action, however, sets it above most other pistols of its size.

Calibre .45 ACP
Type Light double-action only
Overall length 7in
Barrel length 3.5in
Weight 32oz
Sights Combat, tritium night sights
Cartridge capacity 7+1 rounds

The P-12 is quite compact yet has a double-column magazine to offer high capacity. As a result, someone carrying this pistol as a concealed weapon has thirteen rounds available even without a spare magazine. The author has used this size Para-Ordnance quite a lot and has found the grip surprisingly comfortable, despite the fact it is relatively short. In fact, even when firing heavy .45 ACP combat loads, he has not found the recoil uncomfortable in this pistol. Note, too, that the weapon the author has used most often had an alloy frame (an option no longer offered) and, thus, was lighter than the current stainless steel P-12 which should have magnified recoil. For the combination of concealment and high capacity the P-12 is hard to beat.

Calibre .45 ACP
Type Single-action semi-auto
Overall length 7.1in
Barrel length 3.5in
Weight 34oz
Sights Combat, white dots
Cartridge capacity 12+1 rounds

This is the latest incarnation of the Para-Ordnance high-capacity auto-loader introduced in 1990. Available in blued steel or stainless steel, the P-14 not only offers a fourteen-round magazine capacity but also a grip which is surprisingly slim, beaver-tail safety and flared ejection ports among other features. In the Limited version, the P-14 incorporates a match-grade barrel, adjustable sights and ambidextrous safety. The P-14 ranks as one of the world's great combat pistols.

Calibre .45 ACP
Type Single-action semi-auto
Overall length 8.5in
Barrel length 5in
Weight 40oz
Sights Combat or adjustable
   (Limited model)
Cartridge capacity 14+1 rounds

Para-Ordnance Tac-Four

This Para-Ordnance pistol is the author's favourite in size. Though more compact than the full-sized P-14, the Tac-Four still has a magazine capacity of thirteen rounds. It features the light double-action, as well as the bobbed hammer and grip safety. In combination, this makes for an excellent high-capacity concealed-carry weapon. Its size is also such that military or police personnel who must be armed at all times may carry it overtly when in uniform or covertly when in plain clothes. The author considers this to be Para-Ordnance's most versatile combat pistol.

Calibre .45 ACP
Type Light double-action only semi-auto
Overall length 7.7in
Barrel length 4.25in
Weight 36oz
Sights Combat, white dot
Cartridge capacity 13+1 rounds

The CZ 40B is designed to give the grip feel of a Colt 1911A1 but retain the traditional CZ DA/SA trigger system. This pistol does feel good in the hand and like all CZ products functions reliably. On the other hand, most people who want a gun that feels like a Colt 1911A1 will buy a Colt 1911A1. Traditionally, the CZ 75 market has been for those who like the feel of the Browning Hi-Power but want a double-action option.

CZ 40B (C&S Metall-Werkes)

Calibre .40 S&W
Type Double-action semi-auto
Overall length 8.1in
Barrel length 4.7in
Weight 35oz
Sights Front post, rear low-profile square notch
Cartridge capacity 12+1 rounds

CZ 61E (Skorpion)

Czech Republic

Although the Skorpion is a machine pistol, it might more accurately be classified as a compact submachine gun, while the Glock 18 is a true machine pistol. The Skorpion has seen wide usage among Third World police and military forces as well as some terrorist groups. The fact that it incorporates an easily stowed butt stock is a plus but, even so, this is a large pistol, especially for such an anaemic chambering. The Skorpion is available with a suppressor, a feature which makes the .32 ACP chambering more appealing. Cyclic rate with the .32 ACP version is about 700rds/min with a muzzle velocity of 850ft/sec but the small-calibre cartridge makes it reasonably controllable.

CZ 61E Skorpion (C&S Metall-Werkes)

Calibre .32 ACP, .380 and 9mm Makarov
Type Machine pistol
Overall length 10.6in (with stock folded)
Barrel length 4.5in
Weight 45oz
Sights Front post with ears, rear flip adjustable for windage
Cartridge capacity 10 or 20 rounds

The CZ 75 is justifiably one of the world's most popular combat autos. From French detectives to Russian VIP-protection personnel and Rhodesian special forces soldiers it has been the choice of professionals. One of the best features of the CZ 75 is that its grip is very comfortable despite being wide enough for a high-capacity, double-column magazine. Reportedly, the Czech engineers who designed this pistol based the grip on the FN Hi-Power's, one of the best ever designed for instinctive shooting. Another desirable feature of the CZ 75 is that you can carry it as a double-action auto for the first round or can carry it as a single-action auto in cocked-and-locked mode. The only problem with this versatility is that on some models, when carrying the pistol in the double-action mode, the hammer must be lowered by pulling the trigger and riding it forward with the thumb, thus presenting a potential safety problem.

Calibre 9mm and .40 S&W
Type Double-action or single-action semi-auto
Overall length 8.1in
Barrel length 4.7in
Weight 39.5oz
Sights Front blade, rear square notch
Cartridge capacity 15+1 rounds (9mm)

CZ 75D PCR Compact

This pistol, which has been adopted by the Czech National Police, has a lot of features that make it a very appealing combat pistol. Its alloy frame, shorter barrel and shorter grip make it more concealable than the larger CZ 75 pistols, yet it remains a viable weapon for either uniformed or plain-clothes personnel. Unlike the standard CZ 75 which has a safety but not a de-cocker, the PCR incorporates a de-cocker. For military or police use, its lanyard loop is a desirable feature as is the loaded chamber indicator. The rubber grips allow a sure hold even when the hands are moist from rain or perspiration.

Calibre 9mm
Type Double-action semi-auto
Overall length 7.2in
Barrel length 3.8in
Weight 24oz
Sights Fixed, combat
Cartridge capacity 13+1 rounds

CZ 83

Many of the comments about the CZ 75 apply to the scaled-down CZ 83. One of the better high-capacity, medium-powered automatics, the CZ 83 is probably most effective in 9mm Makarov chambering. In fact, the CZ 82 in this calibre was the Czech military pistol for many years when Czechoslovakia was part of the Warsaw Pact.

Calibre .32 ACP, .380 ACP and 9mm Makarov
Type Double-action or single-action semi-auto
Overall length 6.8in
Barrel length 3.8in
Weight 28oz
Sights Front post, rear square notch
Cartridge capacity 13+1 rounds (.380 and 9mm Makarov)

CZ 85 Combat

The CZ 85 is basically the CZ 75 with an ambidextrous safety and ambidextrous slide release. The CZ 85 Combat model incorporates other improvements, including an adjustable rear sight, adjustable trigger and free-fall magazine. This model is also available in satin nickel as illustrated, a feature which increases durability somewhat.

Calibre 9mm
Type Double-action or single-action auto
Overall length 8.1in
Barrel length 4.7in
Weight 35oz
Sights Adjustable
Cartridge capacity 15+1 rounds

Basically a scaled-up CZ 75 for those who like the .45 ACP round, the CZ 97 loses much of the CZ 75's handling characteristics as the grip feels quite thick. Still, it is a highly reliable .45 automatic offering double-action first-round capability. The primary market for this pistol seems to be the USA where the long service of the .45 ACP round has made it extremely popular.

Calibre .45 ACP
Type Double-action or single-action semi-auto
Overall length 8.3in
Barrel length 4.8in
Weight 41.5oz
Sights Front post, rear square notch
Cartridge capacity 10+1 rounds

CZ 100   Czech Republic

The CZ 100 is an entirely new design intended to incorporate many of the most popular innovations in handguns over the last decade. This combines a polymer frame, ergonomic design with no protruding parts, double-action only trigger mechanism and a grip designed for a comfortable hold. The CZ 100 is intended to compete with the Glock and other high-tech designs. As this is written, it is one of the pistols which will take part in trails to select a new French service pistol.

CZ 100 (C&S Metall-Werkes)

Calibre 9mm and .40 S&W
Type Double-action only semi-auto
Overall length 7.1in
Barrel length 3.9in
Weight 24oz
Sights Front blade, rear adjustable notch
Cartridge capacity 13+1 rounds (9mm)

Manurhin MR73 France

France's MR73 is one of the world's best combat revolvers, well proven in serving with such counter-terrorist units as France's GIGN and Austria's GEK Cobra. Designed for durability using very high quality steels, MR73s have been known to fire in excess of 100,000 rounds. Through the use of various sizes of grip as well as a trigger shoe, the MR73 may be configured to fit the individual shooter. Trigger pull is also adjustable by the shooter. The MR73 is very reliable and accurate and deserves its popularity among aficionados of fine handguns. The author is a great fan of the MR73 but does have one criticism of its rear sight. Although the sights are good from a shooting standpoint, the rather large rear blade does have a tendency to catch on the lining of a jacket when the weapon is worn concealed. An auxiliary 9mm cylinder is available for the MR73.

Calibre .357 magnum
Type Double-action revolver
Overall length 9.2in
Barrel length 4in
Weight 37oz
Sights Front ramp, rear adjustable
Cartridge capacity 6 rounds

Manurhin Special Police F1 France

The F1 is the fixed-sight police service Manurhin. Although still of high-quality manufacture, the F1 is designed for mass production at a competitive price. Because it is a service revolver which may be used by maritime units and others where resistance to corrosion is important, the F1 is available in stainless steel as well as blued steel. This 3in-barrelled version is most widely used by French police. As with the MR73, an auxiliary 9mm cylinder is available to allow less expensive shooting with the 9×19 round. The F1 is available only for official sales but the M88 which has a slightly better finish is available for commercial sales. Both the F1 and M88 owe some of their design to the Ruger revolver.

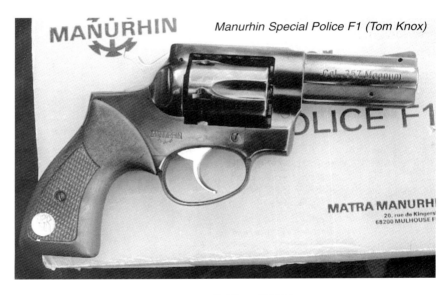

Manurhin Special Police F1 (Tom Knox)

Calibre .357 Magnum
Type Double-action revolver
Overall length 8.1in
Barrel length 3in
Weight 33.5oz
Sights Front ramp, rear notch
Cartridge capacity 6 rounds

Heckler & Koch Mk 23 SOCOM   Germany

The Mk 23 was developed for the US Special Operations Command (SOCOM) as a pistol offering the stopping power of the .45 ACP with match-grade accuracy, rugged durability and large magazine capacity. Prior to deliveries starting to SOCOM in 1996, this pistol went through a battery of rigorous testing. It is a large pistol but that is partially because it has the capability of taking a sound suppressor as well as an assortment of lights, lasers and infrared illuminators. The trigger guard is oversized to allow ease of operation while wearing gloves. The Mk 23 is a specialised pistol designed for special forces and combat swimmers who are willing to accept its bulk in exchange for its wide range of capabilities.

Heckler & Koch Mk 23 SOCOM (T.J. Mullin)

Calibre .45 ACP
Type Double-action or single-action semi-auto
Overall length 9.65in
Barrel length 5.9in
Weight 40oz
Sights Front post, rear square notch, 3-dot night sights available
Cartridge capacity 12+1 rounds

Heckler & Koch P7M8 Germany

The P7 was a very revolutionary design when it was introduced two decades ago. The squeeze-cocker trigger allowed the weapon to be carried entirely safely without the need for a manually operated safety since the weapon remained safe until it was squeezed by the shooting hand to cock the striker. Should the gun fall from the hand, it was immediately rendered safe. This system also allowed a consistently smooth trigger pull which enhanced accuracy. The slide remains open when a magazine is empty and can be released by the same squeeze-cocker. All of these features are quite interesting and, in the hands of a well-trained user, extremely efficient.

Those who have trained military or police personnel with this pistol have found, however, that it can lead to certain safety problems. Users who are not extremely well trained to be constantly aware of the pistol have a tendency to commit two breeches of safety protocols. Anyone using the P7 must be constantly aware of moving while keeping the squeeze-cocker

depressed and of attempting to re-holster the pistol with it depressed: both must be avoided. These mistakes have led to a substantial number of accidental discharges with this pistol.

The P7 is also somewhat top heavy because of its short barrel in relation to the grip. As a result, a proper holster must be chosen which will retain the gun. The P7 remains a very effective pistol in the hands of someone who is well trained with it. However, the author always stresses that any military or police unit using the P7 must be restricted to using just this pistol and no other as switching back and forth can cause users to get sloppy in safety precautions. A double-column version of the P7, the P7M13, has been produced but the grip is so thick that it makes proper use of this pistol more difficult. There has also been a .40 S&W calibre version, the P7M10.

Calibre 9mm
Type Squeeze-cocked semi-auto
Overall length 6.75in
Barrel length 4.15in
Weight 33.5oz
Sights Front post, rear square notch, white dot and outline night sights
Cartridge capacity 8+1 rounds

Heckler & Koch USP

Germany

The USP (Universal Self-Loading Pistol) is H&K's entry into the high-tech police pistol market. It has achieved reasonable success, though certainly not as much as the Glock. The polymer frame helps keep the weight down even on full-sized USPs and the ability to carry it cocked and locked or in double-action mode is appreciated by more sophisticated shooters. On the other hand, it makes the USP less 'cop-proof' since it offers a choice! The USP was one of the first pistols to come with a built-in light or laser rail as standard, a feature now standard on most combat auto-loaders. The USP is quite reliable but the author finds it somewhat boxy in his hand and does not find it a good pistol for instinctive pointing.

Heckler & Koch USP with white-light illuminator attached (T.J. Mullin)

Calibre 9mm and .40 S&W
Type Double-action or single-action semi-auto
Overall length 7.65in
Barrel length 4.25in
Weight 27oz (in 9mm)
Sights Front blade, rear adjustable square notch
Cartridge capacity 15+1 rounds (9mm)

Heckler & Koch USP LEM

Germany

The LEM (Law Enforcement Modified), a compact weapon, is the author's favourite among the current crop of H&K fighting handguns. It is compact, accurate, reliable and safe and has a high magazine capacity. Its action uses the rear movement of the slide for pre-cocking so that the double-action pull can be between 4.5lb and 8lb, depending on what the user or the official agency issuing the weapon finds desirable. This pistol has already been adopted by the US Customs Service and other agencies. Though compact, the LEM incorporates rails for a light or laser, adding even more versatility.

Calibre .40 S&W
Type Double-action only semi-auto
Overall length 7.1in
Barrel length 3.6in
Weight 26oz
Sights Front post, rear notch,
   3-dot or tritium night sights
Cartridge capacity 12+1 rounds

Korth Combat Magnum

The Korth is arguably the world's finest revolver, with a price to match. Each of these revolvers is virtually custom made, with production perhaps of a few hundred per year. Among the special features of the Korth are an easily removable cylinder for cleaning or change to the auxiliary 9mm cylinder. Trigger pull may be adjusted to fit the individual shooter's needs. The combination of a barrel rib and a weighted under-barrel lug make the Korth very controllable in double-action shooting. Another interesting feature is the Korth's cylinder release which is a lever located next to the hammer. This allows the thumb to release the cylinder a bit more readily than on a conventional revolver but this location was dictated by all of the small parts within the frame which did not leave room for a conventional cylinder release. The Korth is a very accurate revolver but it would not justify its high expense for most combat applications.

Calibre .357 Magnum
(auxiliary 9mm cylinder available)
Type Double-action revolver
Overall length 9in
Barrel length 4in
Weight 34.5oz
Sights Front post, rear adjustable
Cartridge capacity 6 rounds

Walther P99 Germany

The P99 is one of the best of the new generation of combat automatics. Its double-action/single-action system allows you to have the light single-action pull for precision shooting or convert to double-action for the first shot by pressing a de-cocking lever built into the top of the slide. The double-action pull runs at about 10lb, while the single-action pull runs at about 5.5lb. Ergonomics are good with an ambidextrous magazine release and a choice of three grip backstraps to fit the gun to the individual user's hand. Both a loaded chamber indicator and a cocking indicator, each of which may be checked visually or by feel, are incorporated. The author has done a substantial amount of shooting with the P99 and has carried it as well. He has found it accurate and reliable and rates it an excellent combat choice. Walther offers basically the same pistol in double-action only format as the P990. Smith & Wesson also produces the P99 through a licensing agreement with Walther.

Walther Model P99

Calibre 9mm, .40 S&W
Type Single-action/double-action striker-fired semi-auto
Overall length 7.1in
Barrel length 4in
Weight 25oz
Sights Front post with white dot, rear windage adjustable square notch with white dots
Cartridge capacity 16+1 rounds (9mm)

Walther PPK

Germany

Perhaps best known as James Bond's favourite pistol, the PPK still ranks as one of the world's best pocket pistols after three-quarters of a century. Compact, reliable and accurate, in current versions it will function with high-performance .380 ammunition. The PPK is available in both stainless steel and blued steel, the former being the most popular choice for enhanced durability. The PPK is also still available in .32 ACP chambering, though most choose the more powerful .380 unless they live in a country where laws dictate that civilians use .32-calibre or lower calibre weapons. The PPK normally comes with two magazine, one with a flat base plate and the other with a finger-extension base plate. The latter holds one more round. Normally, for carrying in a pocket the flat magazine will be carried in the gun while the higher capacity magazine is carried as a reload. Although the PPK was made with an alloy frame in .32 ACP calibre prior to and during the Second World War and for a time after the war, this version is no longer available. This is unfortunate as with contemporary alloys such a lighter PPK would be even better for carrying in a pocket.

Walther Model PPK

Calibre .380
Type Double-action semi-auto
Overall length 6.3in
Barrel length 3.4in
Sights Front post with red dot, rear square notch with red line
Cartridge capacity 6+1 rounds (7+1 with finger-extension magazine)

Beretta Model 21 Bobcat

The Beretta Model 21 and the larger Model 3032 Tomcat in .32 ACP are very popular as self-defence weapons and back-up weapons for police officers in the United States. The combination of a double-action trigger mechanism as well as a safety that allows the pistol to be carried cocked and locked if desired make this small auto quite versatile. It is also a popular lady's self-defence weapon as it incorporates a tip-up barrel that allows the first round to be loaded without having to pull back the slide, a boon for those without strong hands.

Calibre .22 LR and .25 ACP
Type Double-action semi-auto
Overall length 4.9in
Barrel length 2.4in
Weight 11.8oz (.22 LR)
Sights Front blade, rear V-notch
Cartridge capacity 7+1 rounds (.22 LR),
    8+1 rounds (.25 ACP)

Beretta Model 92/M9 Italy

In service with US armed forces, the French *Gendarmerie Nationale* and various other military and police agencies, the Beretta 92 is one of today's best combat auto-loading pistols. Although both the US and French had some initial problems with slides breaking due to the heat treatment, once the problem was fixed, this has proved to be quite a durable service pistol. A stainless steel version is available, offering greater resistance to corrosion. The standard version incorporates a hammer-drop safety on the slide but double-action only versions are available as well, as is the G model which was developed for the French *Gendarmerie*. This version has a variant of the de-cocker safety which returns to the up position after dropping the hammer. In effect, this is really just a de-cocker. This option was provided on the French pistols to preclude the possibility of a user forgetting to remove the safety in a crisis. Unlike many large-capacity auto-loaders, the Beretta 92 feels quite comfortable in the hand and allows good instinctive shooting.

Calibre 9mm and .40 S&W
Type Double-action semi-auto
Overall length 8.5in
Barrel length 4.9in
Weight 34.4oz
Sights Front ramp, rear square notch, night sights available
Cartridge capacity 15+1 rounds (9mm)

Beretta Cougar

Unlike the Beretta 92, the Cougar does not use an open-topped slide and uses a rotating-barrel locking system. As with other Beretta models, the Cougar is available in conventional double-action or double-action only versions. The G model which does not allow the de-cocking lever to also function as a safety is also available. The Cougar has the advantage of taking a full-sized Beretta magazine while offering a slightly more concealable weapon due to the shorter barrel. The closed slide should also have some appeal, especially in areas where sand or other material must be kept out of the weapon's innards.

Beretta Cougar (Trail Creek Trade Company)

Calibre 9mm and .40 S&W
Type Double-action or double-action only semi-auto
Overall length 7.2in
Barrel length 3.6in
Weight 32oz
Sights Front blade, rear square notch
Magazine capacity 15+1 rounds (9mm)

Vanad P-83

Poland

This Polish pistol is sometimes known as the Banard. It was designed as a police and military pistol in 9mm Makarov that was more compact than the P-64. This pistol makes great use of stampings to lower its cost but retains many features of the Makarov and P-64. As with many of the older weapons developed in Poland during the era of the Warsaw Pact, this pistol will most likely be phased out for one in 9×19 to be consistent with Poland's membership in NATO.

Vanad P-83 (T.J. Mullin)

Calibre 9×18 (Makarov)
Type Double-action semi-auto
Overall length 6.5in
Barrel length 3.5in
Weight 25.7oz
Sights Front blade, rear notch
Cartridge capacity 8+1 rounds

PM/PMM

The PSM, or Makarov as it is often known, has been the standard Russian police and military pistol for almost half a century and has proved itself to be very reliable. The PM's design owes much to the Walther PP which the Soviets copied and added a few improvements. The PM is a blowback design but uses the more powerful 9×18 round. There is also an improved Makarov design, the PMM, which has a twelve-round magazine capacity and delayed blowback operation which allows the use of a round within the ballistic range of the 9mm Parabellum. The greatest advantage of the PM from the Russian point of view is that it is relatively simple to manufacture and to train personnel to use. It is also compact enough for it to be carried both overtly and covertly.

Calibre 9mm Makarov
Type Double-action semi-auto
Overall length 6.3in
Barrel length 3.7in
Weight 25.7oz
Sights Front post, rear notch
Cartridge capacity 8+1 rounds

The PSM was introduced into the Soviet Armoury in 1975. At first, Western intelligence agencies could not understand the rationale behind a combat pistol firing such a small cartridge but, when tests proved that the 5.45×18 round would penetrate body armour very readily, it was understood that this pistol was designed to defeat Kevlar body armour and helmets. The PSM is very slim with any controls inset to avoid widening the pistol's profile. As a result, the PSM is a very concealable pistol which can punch through body armour. The PSM seems to be only issued to very specialised military units and has not replaced the PM to any great extent.

Calibre 5.45×18
Type Double-action semi-auto
Overall length 6.1in
Barrel length 3.3in
Weight 16oz
Sights Front blade, rear notch
Cartridge capacity 8+1 rounds

Vektor SP1

Adopted for the South African armed forces, the SP1 incorporates an ambidextrous safety and a reversible magazine release button to make it usable by both right-handed and left-handed shooters. The wraparound grip also makes the SP1 compatible for those with smaller hands. Even though the frame is constructed of alloy, the SP1 is still relatively heavy, though for a military holster pistol this is not a great problem – at least, it is not unless you are an infantryman already carrying nearly 100lb when every ounce is important. Although the SP1 seems a good service pistol, there is really nothing to set it apart from many other 9mm designs.

Vektor SP1 (T.J. Mullin)

Calibre 9mm
Type Double-action semi-auto
Overall length 8.3in
Barrel length 4.65in
Weight 35oz
Sights Front blade, rear square notch, tritium night sights
Cartridge capacity 15+1 rounds

Daewoo DP51 Mk II South Korea (ROK)

The Daewoo uses a rather interesting 'Tri-Action' which allows a light, smooth pull for a first round fired double action. However, the pistol may also be fired as a conventional double-action auto as well. The Daewoo is also available in a compact version and in .40 S&W. This South Korean design is actually quite good and has achieved substantial sales, especially since it is quite reasonably priced when compared with the handguns of many Western producers.

Daewoo DP51 MkII (T. J. Mullin)

Calibre 9mm
Type Double-action semi-auto
Overall length 7.5in
Barrel length 4.1in
Weight 28oz
Sights Front blade, rear square notch
Cartridge capacity 13+1 rounds

Llama M82 Spain

This pistol was adopted by the Spanish Army in 1987 and is a fairly conventional double-action auto, though it does use a dropping-block locking system of the type used in the Walther P38 rather than the more common Browning-style dropping-barrel system. This pistol is available with an alloy frame which would make it much easier to carry.

Llama M-82 (Rene Smeets)

Calibre 9mm
Type Double-action semi-auto
Overall length 8.2in
Barrel length 4.5in
Weight 39oz (steel frame)
Sights Front blade, rear square notch
Cartridge capacity 15+1 rounds

SIG P210 Switzerland

The SIG P210 has now been around for over half a century and was superseded as the Swiss military pistol more than a quarter of a century ago. It is large for a 9×19, has only a single-column magazine and a butt magazine release. At best, it has average sights, incorporates a thumb safety that is very hard to operate until well broken in and is a single-action design in the age of double-actions and fast-action autos. Having listed all of these potential deficiencies, the author can state that he considers the P210 to be the world's best automatic pistol. Many others share this belief. The P210 is made to very high standards and due to a precision barrel and excellent trigger pull it is normally very accurate.

The author has used a P210 as his 'long-range' combat handgun for many years, choosing it for situations when a rifle would probably be more desirable but when he was limited to a handgun. The P210 allows accurate engagement of man-sized targets to at least 100yd. The P210's price tag matches its superb quality. In the past, it has been used by various police and military units which

appreciated its good features. It has now been superseded by more modern pistols in virtually every case, however.

Calibre 9mm
Type Single-action semi-auto
Overall length 8.5in
Barrel length 4.8in
Weight 32oz
Sights Front post, rear square notch
Cartridge capacity 8+1 rounds

SIG P220　　　　　　　　　　　　**Switzerland**

The P220 was the original SIG double-action auto. In 9mm calibre, it replaced the P210 as the official Swiss military pistol. In the USA, the P220 has always been most popular in .45 ACP chambering, though a small recent run in .38 Super calibre has garnered interest. Currently, in addition to blued and two-tone finishes, the P220 is also available in all stainless steel, though this raises the gun's weight by 11.5oz as the stainless frame replaces the alloy frame on the original version. Although the P220 is not the most popular double-action .45 automatic pistol because of its relatively high price, it is one of those pistols that is much valued by its adherents. Many users of the P220 have carried the same pistol for a decade or longer with no urge whatsoever to replace it with something else. The author had a friend, an FBI agent, who started carrying a P220 as soon as it was approved for agents and strapped it on everyday until he retired; it probably remains on his bedside table to this day.

Calibre .45 ACP, limited run in .38 Super
Type Double-action semi-auto
Overall length 7.8in
Barrel length 4.4in
Weight 27.8oz
Sights Front post, rear square notch, white dot and post or tritium night sights
Cartridge capacity 8+1 rounds

The P226 is SIG's most popular double-action auto-loader and has achieved wide success among military and police organisations. Light enough and compact enough to be carried overtly or covertly, the SIG retains traditional SIG accuracy. The .357 SIG and .40 S&W versions are slightly heavier so that they can handle the more powerful cartridges but they are otherwise the same as the basic pistol. The P226 uses a de-cocking lever rather than a manual safety but a double-action only model is available for those agencies that do not want a pistol that can have a cocked hammer, a loaded chamber and no safety applied. P226s have been available in blue, K-coat, nickel and two-tone. The P226 exhibits an excellent balance between safety ergonomics and accuracy.

Calibre 9mm, .357 SIG and .40 S&W
Type Double-action semi-auto
Overall length 7.7in
Barrel length 4.4in
Weight 26.5oz
Sights Front post, rear square notch, white dot and post or tritium night sights
Cartridge capacity 15+1 rounds (in 9mm)

Designed initially as the .40 S&W version of the SIG double-action pistol, the P229 is slightly more compact than the P226 but has a heavier and thicker slide to deal with the heavier .40 S&W round. Since the .357 SIG round is based on the .40 S&W necked down, this was also originally the standard pistol in this calibre, though other SIGs are now chambered for this high-speed cartridge as well. Most of the comments about the P226 apply to the P229 which is also available in double-action only and in nickel, Nitron and two-tone finishes. Although the author likes the P229, some shooters find that it does not balance in the hand quite as well as the P226.

Calibre .40 S&W, 9mm and .357 SIG
Type Double-action semi-auto
Overall length 7.1in
Barrel length 3.9in
Weight 30.5oz
Sights Front post, rear square notch, white dot and post or tritium night sights
Magazine Capacity 12+1 rounds (.40 S&W)

SIG P239

Switzerland

The P239 was developed to give those government agencies that use the SIG a thinner, more concealable option. Hence, the width of the P239 is only 1.2in. As with the larger SIGs, the P239 is very well made and quite accurate. It is available in double-action only format as well as conventional double-action. As its grip is substantially slimmer than the P226 and P229, the P239 is often the choice of smaller people who want a SIG combat auto but are not comfortable with the larger grips. The author finds the P226 grip more comfortable then either the P229 or P239. As with Goldilocks and the three bears' beds, one is too big, one is too small and the other is just right! That is, of course, the reason that many manufacturers of combat pistols offer different sizes, since the pistol must fit the hand of the shooter for it to be used most effectively.

Calibre 9mm, .357 SIG and .40 S&W
Type Double-action semi-auto
Overall length 6.6in
Barrel length 3.6in
Weight 27.4oz
Sights Front post, rear square notch, white
dot and post or tritium night sights
Cartridge capacity 8+1 rounds (9mm)

SIG P245   Switzerland

The P245 is SIG's compact .45 ACP auto-loader. It will take the same magazine as the larger P220, thus allowing it to be used as a compact back-up gun for the larger .45 ACP pistol. As with other SIG double-action autos, the P245 may be ordered with double-action only if so desired. Finishes include Nitron and Ilaflon as well as two-tone. Just as the P220 is one of the most accurate of all .45 automatics, the P245 is quite accurate as well, especially for its compact size.

SIG P245 (C&S Metall-Werkes)

Calibre .45 ACP
Type Double-action semi-auto
Overall length 7.2in
Barrel length 3.9in
Weight 27.5oz
Sights Front blade, rear square notch, white dot and post or tritium night sights
Cartridge capacity 6+1 rounds

SIG Pro SP2340

The SIG Pro is the latest generation SIG auto-loading pistol. In addition to its integral fire control system, the SIG Pro utilises a polymer frame with an integral accessory rail for a laser or white light. Assorted grips and triggers are available to fit the pistol to the individual user. A great selling point for law enforcement agencies is the SIG Pro's 'four-point safety system': automatic firing pin lock; de-cocking lever; safety intercept notch; trigger bar disconnector. It is available in Nitron finish or in two-tone.

The SIG Pro has gained a substantial cachet in the USA since its adoption by both the Secret Service and the FAA Air Marshals in .357 SIG calibre. Various other federal, state and local law enforcement agencies have adopted it as well. The SIG Pro has just won the French police trials, too. Although the SIG Pro has incorporated many of the features considered necessary on the latest combat autos, it has retained traditional SIG accuracy. Reportedly, it is very accurate with the .357 SIG cartridge, one reason agencies such as the Secret Service and the Air Marshals, which put great stress on precision shooting, have adopted it.

Calibre .40 S&W, 9mm and .357 SIG
Type Double-action semi-auto (convertible via integral fire control to DAO)
Overall length 7.4in
Barrel length 3.9in
Weight 28oz
Sights Front post, rear square notch, white dot and post or tritium night sights
Cartridge capacity 12 rounds

Autauga Mk II

Like the Seecamp which will be discussed later, the Autauga is designed as a hideout gun to shoot high-performance .32 ACP ammunition. The Autauga has a sleek profile to lessen the chance of catching it on anything while drawing it from a pocket. The use of the DAO action precludes the need for any external safeties, thus speeding initial engagement and eliminating a possible protrusion to snag on clothing during the draw. The magazine release is at the base of the magazine, not generally considered the optimum location for rapid changes, but it is a location that is less likely to result in the magazine inadvertently being released in a pocket. Additionally, this is not a weapon designed for an extended gunfight where a magazine change would be necessary. This pistol is intended for close-range engagement in dire circumstances. The Autauga does incorporate rudimentary sights but this is still basically a pistol for use at 10yd or less.

Calibre .32 ACP
Type Double-action semi-auto
Overall length 4.8in
Barrel length 2.3in
Weight 12oz
Sights Front post, rear notch
Cartridge capacity 6+1 rounds

Colt 1991-A1 (Government Model) USA

Though almost a century old, this John Browning design is still considered one of the world's best combat pistols. It is highly reliable and with its large .45-calibre bullet a proven stopper. With a bit of work to accurise it, the Government Model is also one of the most accurate pistols. The National Match version is specifically designed for target competition but has also been used for combat by those wanting greater accuracy. The combination of a thumb safety and a grip safety also make this a more 'soldier-proof' weapon than some others. Many of those who like the Government Model actually prefer the Commander version which has a barrel $3/4$ in shorter and an alloy frame. More readily carried concealed, some consider this the ultimate combat auto. There is also an even smaller Officer's Model.

Colt 1991-A1 (Trail Creek Trade Company)

Calibre .45 ACP, .38 Super and 9mm
Type Single-action semi-auto
Overall length 8.5in
Barrel length 5in
Weight 39.5oz
Sights Front post, rear square notch
Cartridge capacity 7+1 rounds

The Python is generally viewed as one of the world's best revolvers. It is extremely accurate and well made but is also quite heavy. The weight does, however, help control recoil and muzzle flip with the .357 Magnum round. The Python has been offered with 2.5in, 3in, 4in, 6in and 8in barrels. For combat, however, the 4in version has always been most popular. Known for its lustrous bluing, the Python has also been offered in nickel as well as matt and bright stainless steel. For many years, the Python was a status symbol among US police officers who carried it because of its cachet. Unfortunately, the Python has always been substantially more expensive than many of its competitors which has limited its market.

Colt Python, Class D engraved

Calibre .357 Magnum
Type Revolver
Overall length 9.5in
Barrel length 4in
Weight 47.5oz
Sights Front ramp on ventilated rib, rear adjustable
Cartridge capacity 6 rounds

Downsizer WSP

The WSP designation of this tiny pistol stands for World's Smallest Pistol. Designed to be a hideout gun for undercover police officers or others who need ultimate concealment, the WSP is well made but the design features stress compactness. When testing this pistol, the author found that it could be hidden in a cigarette packet or box, an indication of how small it really is. The Downsizer does, however, have a serious downside. Since it is chambered for very serious combat pistol cartridges and is so small and light, recoil is punishing. To give an idea just how bad it is, the author has often fired a hundred rounds of full-power .44 Magnum ammunition in one shooting session but the most he could fire when testing the Downsizer was four rounds spread over an hour. The most punishing part of shooting this tiny pistol is that the trigger guard and trigger violently whack your finger as it recoils. Though an interesting design, the Downsizer will be chosen by few as a combat pistol.

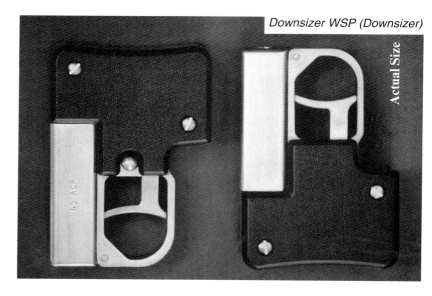

Downsizer WSP (Downsizer)

Actual Size

Calibre .357 Magnum and .45 ACP
Type Double-action only, single-shot derringer
Overall length 3.25in
Barrel length 2.1in
Weight 11oz
Sights None
Cartridge capacity 1 round

Kahr MK40

Kahr Arms pistols are designed to offer excellent power in a compact concealment pistol. Kahr pistols are also very reliable and accurate. Kahr uses an offset-barrel system which places the trigger mechanism beside the barrel lug, thus raising the shooter's hand nearer to the centre line of the bore. This combined with the very ergonomic grips allows the Kahr to be surprisingly comfortable to shoot despite its compact size. The double-action cocking-cam trigger action is quite smooth and allows the Kahr to be used more accurately than many double-action only pistols.

The Kahrs are normally supplied with two magazine, one with a flat base for concealment and one with grip extension that allows an extra cartridge to be loaded. Most users carry the pistol with the flat base magazine in place and use the grip extension magazine as the spare. The only criticism the author really has of the Kahr MK40 is that it is a bit heavy for a pocket pistol. However, Kahr has now introduced a line of polymer-framed pistols which are much lighter. In addition to the MK40, there is the larger K40 as well as a full-sized and compact 9mm. The P9 and P40 are polymer-framed versions.

Calibre .40 S&W
Type Double-action only semi-auto
Overall length 6in
Barrel length 3.5in
Weight 23.1oz
Sights Front post, rear notch, white dot and bar night sights
Cartridge capacity 5+1 rounds

Kahr PM9

As with other Kahr Arms pistols, the PM9 is very reliable, very safe, very compact and very accurate. The consistent double-action trigger pull allows good accuracy for such a compact pistol. The PM9 is not only compact but because of its polymer frame it is also very light. This is, in fact, one of the best back-up guns for law enforcement officers who want a light but powerful weapon to carry in a pocket, on an ankle or on a ballistic vest.

Calibre 9mm
Type Double-action only semi-auto
Overall length 5.3in
Barrel length 3in
Weight 14oz
Sights Front post, rear square notch, white dot and bar or tritium night sights
Cartridge capacity 6+1 rounds (7+1 with finger-extension magazine)

Kel-Tec P-32

The Kel-Tec is a very light pistol which employs alloys and polymers. It is designed to be durable enough to reliably handle any .32 ACP round, including special loads. The Kel-Tec is available with blued, Parkerized or chromed metal parts. The double-action trigger mechanism allows the pistol to be carried ready for action without any additional safeties The 6lb pull is not so stiff that it unduly impedes accuracy. Another feature in favour of the Kel-Tec is that it is quite reasonably priced.

Kel-Tec P-32 (C&S Metall-Werkes)

Calibre .32 ACP
Type Double-action only semi-auto
Overall length 5.1in
Barrel length 2.7in
Weight 6.6oz
Sights Front post, rear notch
Cartridge capacity 7+1 rounds

Kel-Tec P-11

The P-11 offers a compact, light, safe 9mm handgun at a very affordable price. Though a very basic design, the Kel-Tec is just as deadly as a 9mm auto at three or four times the price. Whether as a police back-up gun or as a civilian self-defence gun, the Kel-Tec gives excellent value for money. It is available in various finishes, including green.

Kel-Tec P-11 (C&S Metall-Werkes)

Calibre 9mm
Type Double-action only semi-auto
Overall length 5.9in
Barrel length 3.1in
Weight 16.8oz
Sights Front post, rear notch
Cartridge capacity 10+1 rounds

Kimber Classic Royal   USA

Kimber's custom series of full-sized .45 autos incorporate such features as front and rear slide serrations, match-grade trigger group, match-grade barrel, full-length guide rod, extended ambidextrous safety, front grip-strap chequering and match-grade premium aluminium trigger. The purchaser has the choice of black synthetic, chequered walnut or smooth rosewood grips. Finishes available are matt black, high-polish blue or stainless. Kimber's custom series guns are designed to offer superb accuracy and outstanding reliability, both absolutely necessary features in a combat pistol.

Kimber Classic Royal (Trail Creek Trade Company)

Calibre .45 ACP, 9mm, .38 Super and .40 S&W
Type Single-action semi-auto
Overall length 8.7in
Barrel length 5in
Sights Front blade, rear McCormick low profile (normally with tritium night sights)
Cartridge capacity 7+1 rounds (.45 ACP)

Kimber Compact CDP II

Thought to be compact enough for concealed carrying, the Compact CDP II incorporates many features normally only found on full-sized combat autos. These included rounded and bevelled corners to make the pistol more snag-free when drawn from beneath a jacket, tritium night sights, chequered front strap, extended ambidextrous safety, match-grade premium aluminium trigger and hand-chequered, double-diamond rosewood grips. Its alloy frame keeps weight down for ease of carrying as well. In addition to being an accurate and reliable combat handgun, this is also a very handsome one with its two-tone finish and contrasting grips.

Calibre .45 ACP
Type Single-action semi-auto
Overall length 7.7in
Barrel length 4in
Weight 28oz
Sights Combat, tritium night sights
Cartridge capacity 7+1 rounds

Ruger GP100

Perhaps the most striking characteristic of the GP100 is its sturdiness. With its full-length ejector shroud, double-locked cylinder, cylinder-locking notches positioned on the thickest portion of the cylinder, and reinforced frame, this is a revolver which can handle any factory .357 Magnum load with ease. Because the GP100 is comprised of a group of integrated subassemblies, it may be disassembled for maintenance quickly and easily without tools. Since the grip portion of the frame is a peg on to which the grips are fitted, the user may choose easily from several different grip options. The GP100 is available in blued steel or stainless steel. Though a highly reliable and sturdy revolver which handles recoil with ease, the price you pay for all of the GP100's sturdiness is that it is quite heavy when compared to some other .357 Magnum revolvers.

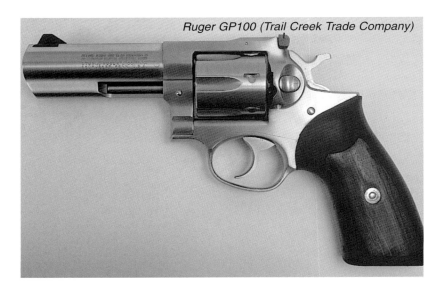

Ruger GP100 (Trail Creek Trade Company)

Calibre .357 Magnum
Type Double-action revolver
Overall length 9.4in
Barrel length 4in
Weight 41oz
Sights Front ramp, rear adjustable
Cartridge capacity 6 rounds

Ruger P90

The P90 is typical in most characteristics of the quite extensive Ruger P series of auto-loading pistols. Other models are available in 9mm and .40 S&W with a choice of manual safety, de-cock only or double-action only. Aluminium frames are used to keep the weight down but as with all Rugers sturdiness and durability are characteristics of the P series of autos. The P90 and other Ruger autos may be quickly and easily stripped to the five primary components for maintenance.

Ruger P90 (Trail Creek Trade Company)

Calibre .45 ACP
Type Double-action semi-auto
Overall length 7.25in
Barrel length 4.5in
Weight 33.5oz
Sights Front post, rear square notch
Cartridge capacity 8+1 rounds

Ruger SP101

The SP101 is relatively heavy for a short-barrelled .357 Magnum and it only holds five rounds but it is known for its sturdiness. Even the hottest .357 Magnum factory loads may be fired confidently in the SP101. The SP101 is known, as well, for its very comfortable ergonomic grips. The combination of the SP101's durability and its stainless steel finish make it an especially good choice for those who keep a revolver near at hand for self-defence, aboard a yacht, for example.

Calibre .357 Magnum
Type Double-action revolver
Overall length 7in
Barrel length 2.25in
Weight 25oz
Sights Front ramp, rear notch
Cartridge capacity 5 rounds

The Seecamp is designed to offer a very high quality, reliable, compact auto for deep concealment. The LWS-32 is designed to be as sleek as possible to allow a rapid draw from the pocket, hence the lack of sights. Since this is a pistol designed for self-defence at very close range, it is intended to be pointed instinctively rather than deliberately aimed. The magazine release is at the bottom of the butt as this position lessons the likelihood of the magazine being released inadvertently while the gun is in the pocket. Fabricated of stainless steel, the LWS-32 is durable enough for carrying in concealment holsters worn close to the body (e.g. bra holsters) by undercover police officers. The LWS-32 is also designed to be very safe. When the magazine is removed, not only is the trigger locked but so is the slide. Early versions of the LWS-32 were designed to be used only with Winchester's .32 ACP Silvertip load. However, current production pistols will function reliably with a wide array of .32 ACP loads.

Calibre .32 ACP
Type Double-action only semi-auto
Overall length 4.25in
Barrel length 2in
Weight 11oz
Sights none
Cartridge capacity 6+1 rounds

Smith & Wesson Model 60

The Model 60 was the original stainless steel handgun which pioneered the use of the corrosion-resistant steel for hundreds of future handguns. Originally a 2in-barrelled .38 Special weighing 19oz, the Model 60 Chief's Special has been beefed up over the last few years to take the .357 Magnum cartridge. Although the resulting handgun offers greater stopping power it is heavier and harder to carry in the pocket. Model 60s have been produced with 3in barrels and with adjustable sights. The niche for a powerful pocket revolver has now been filled by Smith & Wesson's scandium and titanium revolvers.

Calibre .38 Special and .357 Magnum
Type Double-action revolver
Overall length 6. 6in
Barrel length 2.1in
Weight 24oz
Sights Front ramp, rear notch
Cartridge capacity 5 rounds

Smith & Wesson Model 64

As the Smith & Wesson Military and Police Revolver (Model 10), this basic design was one of the world's most popular handguns throughout much of the twentieth century. Offered in various finishes and barrel lengths of 2in, 3in, 4in, 5in and 6in, the Model 10 rode in police and military holsters around the world. There was also an Airweight version having an alloy frame. Designated the Model 12, this revolver carried very easily yet gave its user the power of the .38 Special round. Currently, Smith & Wesson has discontinued the original Model 10 and only offers the design in the stainless steel Model 64 which is available in 2in, 3in and 4in barrels, the first two with a round butt and the latter with a square butt. The Model 64 and its predecessor remain popular weapons with security guards and homeowners, though most law enforcement agencies have traded them in for semi-auto pistols.

Smith & Wesson Model 64, NYPD DAO version (T.J. Mullin)

Calibre .38 Special
Type Double-action revolver
Overall length 8. 8in
Barrel length 4in
Weight 36oz
Sights Front ramp, rear notch
Cartridge capacity 6 rounds

Smith & Wesson Model 66

The Model 66 is the stainless steel version of Smith & Wesson's Model 19 Combat Magnum which pioneered a .357 Magnum revolver that did not need to be as large as had previously been the case. This snub version has always appealed to the author as he has found that he can shoot it very well in double-action, the short barrel seeming to balance just right for rapid follow-up shots. The most popular barrel length, however, has always been the 4in. This revolver is also offered with a 6in barrel, though that length is more popular for sport than combat. For years, the Model 66 has ranked as one of the most versatile of all revolvers since it is light enough to carry concealed yet has good stopping power with the magnum chambering.

There is also a 'service' version with fixed sights designated the Model 65. Because the Model 66 was designed to be easy to carry, there has been some concern that firing many thousands of rounds of full-power .357 Magnum rounds through this medium-framed revolver could cause excessive wear. The Model 686 (see below) was

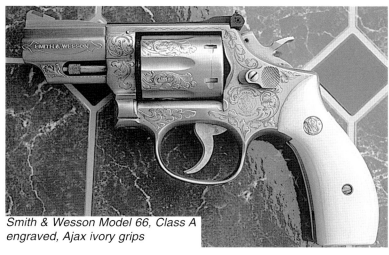

Smith & Wesson Model 66, Class A engraved, Ajax ivory grips

developed to address this problem. One solution adopted by many law enforcement agencies that carried the Model 66 was to practice with .38 Special loads but to carry .357 Magnum loads for duty. Since the author believes that you should practice with the loads you will shoot in combat, he has always shot his Model 66s with full-power .357 Magnum loads and has never had a problem.

Calibre .357 Magnum
Type Double-action revolver
Overall length 7.5in
Barrel length 2.5in
Weight 32oz
Sights Front ramp with red insert, rear adjustable with white outline
Cartridge capacity 6 rounds

Smith & Wesson Model 360PD USA

The 360PD is typical of the latest generation of Smith & Wesson compact revolvers that use scandium and titanium to fabricate incredibly light revolvers, especially when it is considered that this weapon is chambered for the .357 magnum round. The only limitation to the use of .357 Magnum ammunition is that loads with bullets below 110 grains in weight are not recommended, reportedly because 110-grain .357 Magnum JHP loads have a history of flame cutting around the forcing cone. In addition to being very strong, scandium is also rust resistant so the user gets the advantages of stainless steel in a very light revolver. The 360PD is equipped with a lanyard ring built into the butt which allows the pistol to be carried around the neck on a lanyard. This would even allow a soldier or operator in an extremely dangerous combat zone to wear the pistol while in the shower! The 360PD has an exposed hammer, while the 340PD has a shrouded hammer and, hence, must be fired in DAO mode.

Calibre .357 Magnum
Type Double-action revolver
Overall length 6.3in
Barrel length 1. 8in
Weight 12oz
Sights Front ramp with red insert, rear notch
Cartridge capacity 5 rounds

Combining an aluminium alloy frame and a titanium cylinder, the Model 396 offers a big-bore, lightweight weapon. This revolver offers the option of using a larger calibre cartridge than the .357 Magnum scandium guns. However, because of concerns about bullets 'jumping' the case, heavier bullet loads are not recommended. The Cor-Bon 165-grain JHP load works especially well in this revolver. The Model 396 incorporates a lanyard ring for ease of retention. The Model 396 is an especially useful weapon for outdoorsmen or those who work in areas having both two-legged and four-legged dangers. There are two versions of the Model 386 Mountain Lite, offering seven-shot .357 Magnums.

Calibre .44 Special
Type Double-action revolver
Overall length 8.1in
Barrel length 3.1in
Weight 18oz
Sights Front post with HIVIZ green insert, rear adjustable
Cartridge capacity 5 rounds

Smith & Wesson Model 457

This pistol is in Smith & Wesson's Value Series, a no-frills group of service pistols designed for the law enforcement market. In addition to the Model 457, there are also three 9mm and two .40 S&W models in this series. The Model 457 has an alloy frame which makes it an easily carried and concealed .45 auto. This pistol will take the same magazine as the larger Smith & Wesson duty .45 automatics, thus making it a good choice as a back-up to one of the larger autos. Note also that it has a bobbed hammer to lesson the chances of the pistol snagging during a draw from concealment.

Smith & Wesson Model 457 (T.J. Mullin)

Calibre .45 ACP
Type Double-action semi-auto
Overall length 7.3in
Barrel length 3.8in
Weight 29oz
Sights Front post with white dot, rear Novak combat with 2 dots
Cartridge capacity 7+1 rounds

Smith & Wesson Model 686+

The Model 686 revolver, built on Smith & Wesson's L frame, was developed to offer a .357 Magnum revolver sturdy enough to stand up to continuous use with full-powered Magnum loads but which was lighter than revolvers built on the hefty N frame. The addition of a seven-shot cylinder in the '+' models made the Model 686 more competitive with auto-loading pistols by increasing cartridge capacity. The full-length under-barrel lug on the Model 686 helps dampen recoil and aids in quick, double-action shooting. On the other hand, the lug also adds weight. As a result, Smith & Wesson has made a limited number of Model 686+ Mountain Guns which utilise a thinner, lighter barrel. Many experienced shooters consider the Model 686+ Mountain Gun one of the best combat revolvers ever made and the author must admit that he is one of them.

Smith & Wesson Model 686+ Mountain Gun, Eagle Secret Service grips

Calibre .357 Magnum
Type Double-action revolver
Overall length 9.6in
Barrel length 4in
Weight 38.5oz
Sights Front ramp with red insert, rear adjustable with white outline
Cartridge capacity 7 rounds

The Sigma is Smith & Wesson's first entry into the polymer duty pistol market and is designed as a pistol which is easy to carry, very safe, yet ready for instant action. High magazine capacity without unduly increasing the thickness of the grip is another positive feature. The latest generation of Sigmas incorporates a built-in rail for lights or lasers, granting even more versatility to the Sigma. In service, the Sigma has proved to be very durable.

Calibre .40 S&W, 9mm
Type Double-action only semi-auto
Overall length 7.3in
Barrel length 4in
Weight 24.4oz
Sights Front post with white dot or tritium dot, rear square notch with 2 white dots or 2 tritium dots
Cartridge capacity 14+1 rounds (.40 S&W)

Smith & Wesson Model 3953

The Model 39 was Smith & Wesson's original double-action automatic and was the first automatic of this type widely adopted by US law enforcement agencies, including the Illinois State Police and the Salt Lake City Police. The original Model 39 used an alloy frame with a blued steel slide. While the Model 3953 retains the alloy frame, it uses a stainless steel slide and barrel. This pistol is the current incarnation of the Smith & Wesson single-column magazine 9mm. The Model 3953 is double-action only, while the Model 3913 is a traditional double-action. The most recent versions of this pistol are in the TSW (Tactical Smith & Wesson) series and incorporate a rail for lights and lasers on the frame.

Calibre 9mm
Type Double-action only semi-auto
Overall length 6.8in
Barrel length 3.5in
Weight 24.8oz
Sights Front post with white dot,
  rear Novak Lo Mount, 2 dots
Cartridge capacity 8+1 rounds

Smith & Wesson Model 3953 (T.J. Mullin)

REDRAWN 1985
NRA #B-8 (CP)

Smith & Wesson Model 4566 TSW

This is an all stainless steel, full-sized .45 automatic. Among its features are an ambidextrous safety. The Model 4563 is virtually the same pistol but is fabricated with an alloy frame and steel slide, which saves about 9oz in weight. Since this is a TSW model, it incorporates the accessory rail for laser or light. This pistol would normally have a matt stainless steel finish but this is a special order military weapon with Melonite finish and lanyard ring.

Smith & Wesson Model 4566 TSW
with Melonite finish

Calibre .45 ACP
Type Double-action semi-auto
Overall length 7.9in
Barrel length 4.3in
Weight 39.1oz
Sights Front post with white dot, rear
    Novak Lo Mount with 2 dots
Cartridge capacity 8+1 rounds

Smith & Wesson Model 5906

The Model 5906 is an all-stainless-steel, high-magazine capacity 9mm pistol. The original Model 59 was Smith & Wesson's first high-capacity auto and has now been through many incarnations. The pistol illustrated is from a special military contact. Note that it has a lanyard ring. Also, although it is fabricated from stainless steel, there is an additional Melonite coating to give even greater corrosion resistance. Melonite, which is often ordered for pistols for combat swimmers, can stand up to thousands of hours of continuous salt spray without a blemish. This pistol is also currently available in TSW format.

Smith & Wesson Model 5906 with Melonite finish (T.J. Mullin)

Calibre 9mm
Type Double-action semi-auto
Overall length 7.5in
Barrel length 4in
Weight 38.3oz
Sights Front post with white dot, rear Novak Lo Mount with 2 dots
Cartridge capacity 15+1 rounds

Springfield Armory 1911A1 USA

The Springfield Armory version of the venerable 1911A1 offers myriad options. For example, it can be ordered in stainless steel and with a matt blue, Parkerized or green finish. Alloy frames are available as are wide-body frames for high-capacity fourteen-round magazine. 'Chopped' slides and barrels in lengths of 3in or 4in are available. Among custom features are special triggers, skeletonised hammers, front slide serrations and special grip safeties.

Springfield Armory 1911A1 (C&S Metall-Werkes)

Calibre .45 ACP
Type Single-action semi-auto
Overall length 8.6in
Barrel length 5in
Weight 38.5oz
Sights Front post, rear Novak combat, adjustable and tritium night sights
Cartridge capacity 7+1 rounds

Springfield Armory XD-9

The X-Treme Duty is Springfield Armory's entry into the polymer combat pistol arena. It uses the Safety Assurance USA Action Trigger System which is another double-action/fast-action system designed to allow the pistol to be carried ready for immediate action without operating an external safeties. However, the XD does incorporate a grip safety which will immediately render the pistol inoperable should it be dropped. Among other features are an ambidextrous safety and loaded chamber and cocked striker indicators. An accessory rail for light or laser is another useful feature.

Springfield Armory XD-9 (C&S Metall-Werkes)

Calibre 9mm, .40 S&W and .357 SIG
Overall length 7in
Barrel length 4in
Weight 28oz
Sights Front post with white dot, rear notch with white dots
Cartridge capacity 15+1 rounds (9mm)

Suggested Reading

Jordan, Bill, *No Second Place Winner*, Published by the Author (1965)

Keith, Elmer, *Sixguns, The Standard Reference Work*, Bonanza Books (1955)

Konig, Klaus-Peter and Martin Hugo, *A History of the World's 9mm Pistols & Ammunition*, Schiffer Military History (1992)

Konig, Klaus-Peter and Martin Hugo, *Service Handguns A Collector's Guide*, Batsford (1988)

Morrison, Gregory Boyce, *The Modern Technique of the Pistol*, Gunsight Press (1991)

Mullin, Timothy J., *Handbook of Handguns*, Paladin Press (2001)

Mullin, Timothy J., *The 100 Greatest Combat Pistols*, Paladin Press (1994)

Mullin, Capt. Timothy John, *Training the Gunfighter*, Paladin Press (1981)

Nonte, George (ed. Edward C. Ezell), *Combat Handguns*, Stackpole (1980)

Thompson, Leroy and Rene Smeets, *Great Combat Handguns*, Arms & Armour Press (1993)

Wallack, L.R., *American Pistol & Revolver Design and Performance*, Winchester Press (1978)

Zhuk, A.B., *The Illustrated Encyclopaedia of Handguns*, Greenhill (1995)